SOME] Teashop`Walks

Roger Evans

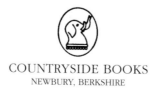

COUNTRYSIDE BOOKS
NEWBURY, BERKSHIRE

First published 2005
© Roger Evans, 2005

COUNTRYSIDE BOOKS
3 Catherine Road
Newbury, Berkshire

To view our complete range of books,
please visit us at
www.countrysidebooks.co.uk

ISBN 1 85306 891 8

Photographs by the author

Designed by Graham Whiteman
Produced through MRM Associates Ltd., Reading
Printed by Arrowsmith, Bristol

Contents

Walk

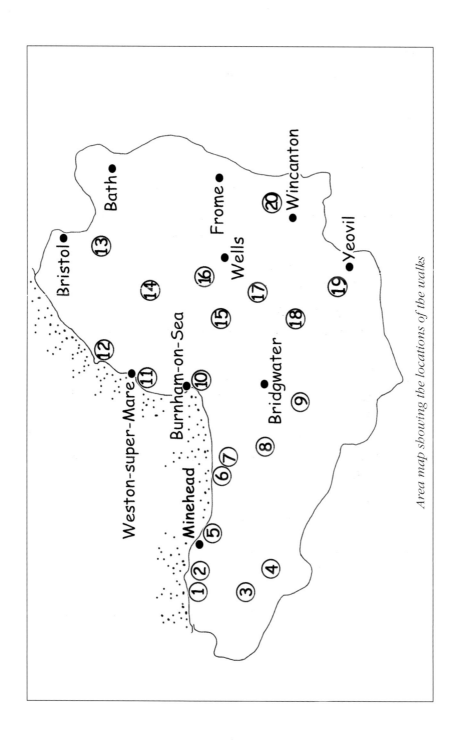

Area map showing the locations of the walks

Introduction

Few counties boast such a range of scenery with footpaths and bridleways ideal for the walker as Somerset. In the west we have glorious Exmoor, rich in teashops and walks that could justify a book on their own. Then there are the Quantock Hills, much loved by Coleridge and Wordsworth who wrote their finest and best-remembered poems here.

In the north are the Mendip Hills with the dramatic grandeur of Cheddar Gorge and the smaller, less visited but equally beautiful Ebbor Gorge. Parts of these hills extend out into the Bristol Channel to provide clifftop walks along coastal headlands. These in turn contrast with the flat moorland of the Somerset Levels, the peat moors of Athelney and the rolling hills of south Somerset.

I have lived and walked in Somerset all my life and yet, whilst preparing this book, I have discovered and explored previously unvisited byways that have added to both my enjoyment and knowledge of my home county. I have become acquainted with some wonderful teashops, some in bustling town centres and others in remote farmhouses deep in Exmoor, and received a warm Somerset welcome at them all.

The walks, which are circular and vary from a stroll of 2½ miles at Sand Bay to slightly longer routes that might encompass lunch as well as tea, can be enjoyed throughout the year. Where a chosen teashop's opening hours are limited, I have suggested an alternative source of refreshment on the route or nearby. I have also given details of car parks that are close to the start of each route; however, if you decide to opt for roadside parking, please be sure that your car doesn't cause an obstruction while you are on your walk.

Throughout my voyage of discovery, during the countless hours of walking through the countryside of Somerset, my constant companion has been Buster, my border collie, and he also has benefited from the experience. Between us, we have found and recorded twenty walks and many more teashops. My grateful thanks go to my eldest son, Gareth, and to my wife, both of whom have tried out a number of these routes.

I trust that you will get as much enjoyment from these walks and these teashops as we did in discovering them.

Roger Evans

Walk 1
HORNER WOODS

The village of Horner, nestling beneath Dunkery Beacon and Webber's Post, is an excellent centre for walking, reflecting the cooperation between the National Trust and the Exmoor National Park Authority. The first section of the route passes over a packhorse bridge to ascend through deciduous woodland, eventually to emerge onto open moorland with good prospects of spotting red deer (which to date I have seen on every visit). The return leg of the walk leads gently downhill, following the occasionally cascading Horner Water. Just before the end of the circuit there is another packhorse bridge, and the presence of two such bridges in such a small community reflects the significance of this hamlet on the packhorse trail to Dunster with its medieval yarn market, a major centre at one time for the wool trade.

☕ Horner Tea Gardens sit peacefully alongside the ancient Horner Woods and the fast flowing Horner Water, with wonderful views up into the valley. There are tables and chairs for over 100 and a covered veranda offers shelter in poor weather. Apart from cream teas and cakes, a range of snacks is available such as ploughman's and filled jacket potatoes. The gardens are open daily, 11 am to 6 pm, from Easter to the end of September, with slightly shorter opening hours from Lady Day (end of March) to Easter, and in October. To confirm the times outside the holiday season, telephone: 01643 862380.

An alternative venue is Horner Vale Tea Gardens, also near the car park. Ploughman's, cream teas, home-made cakes and their speciality meringues are on offer. Telephone: 01643 862506.

During winter months, the Wortleberry Tea Room can be found in the High Street of nearby Porlock, about 1½ miles from the car park at the starting point. It is open all year, dogs are welcomed in the walled patio, and the scones are well recommended. Telephone: 01643 862337.

DISTANCE: 5½ miles.
MAP: OS Outdoor Leisure 9 Exmoor.
STARTING POINT: The free car park at Horner (GR 898454).
HOW TO GET THERE: Horner is signposted to the south off the A39 between Porlock and Minehead, about ¾ mile outside Porlock. The road soon leads you past the caravan park into Horner village where the car park is well marked and easy to find on your left hand side.
ALTERNATIVE STARTING POINT: The car park is large and an alternative should not be necessary. However, the walk could be started either where the path meets the road near Woodcocks Ley (point 8) or at Pool Bridge (point 9) where limited roadside parking can be found. Horner Tea Gardens would then be at approximately the halfway point of the route.

THE WALK

As well as being an ideal walking centre, with many paths radiating out from the village, Horner is also perfect for horse riding and there are stables along one side of the car park. Leaving the car park by the footpath in the corner where the public toilets can be found brings the visitor out onto the road by our chosen teashop. Just across the road is a fine old mill with its own leat running down from Horner Water.

1. To start the walk, leave the car park by the road entrance through which you entered. Turn left.

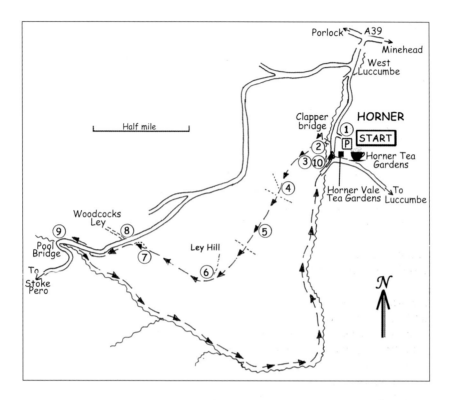

2. Almost immediately, turn right and take the bridleway over the small cobblestoned packhorse bridge. Turn right and in about 20 yards turn right again, signposted 'Cat's Scramble'.

The packhorse bridge is a well-preserved example of its type. It may appear to be unnecessarily steep considering its short distance but herein there is a purpose. During heavy winds and rains, large branches can be swept down the river and the high clearance provided by this design allows them to pass beneath. The sides of the bridge are low to permit the wide loads carried on horseback to pass over undamaged.

3. Pass through a gate and continue uphill along the obvious path.

You will now be ascending the hill through deciduous woodland with magnificent oak trees and many ash trees. Green woodpeckers are abundant here and the call, something like a laughing sound, which earns them the local name of 'yaffle', should be frequently heard.

Pool Bridge crossing Horner Water

4. Ignore the path which goes off to the right and keep straight on when another path crosses yours shortly after.

5. Continue straight ahead when Cat's Scramble merges with Granny's Ride.

At this point a signpost tells you that you have just completed ¾ mile from Horner. Every time I pass this way, I question that distance. It always feels more but take comfort that most of the uphill is now behind you and it is just a gradual upward slope from now on. A couple of benches are conveniently positioned along this stretch of the walk.

At a crossroad of paths, continue straight ahead uphill and join Flora's Ride (signposted) where you will turn right to find the Ley Hill road (signposted).

As you emerge from the trees, keep a watchful eye open for the red deer that are plentiful on Exmoor. Although they can be hard to spot in the woodland, they frequently graze on the open ground and particularly around Ley Hill, which is before you as you come out of the woods and then moves around to your right as you progress.

6. At the T-junction with a dirt road, turn left with Ley Hill on your right.

7. Where the path forks, take the left track (they both come back together) and in a short distance you reach the metalled road.

8. Turn left at the road and follow it all the way down to Pool Bridge where the road crosses Horner Water.

This makes a good halfway point to stop and picnic, if you so wish, alongside the river in the shade of the trees, perhaps having a summertime paddle in the fast flowing water below the bridge. You now have about 2¼ miles to go.

9. Just before the bridge, turn left to follow the river downstream, keeping the river on your right-hand side. The path is well defined and leads you all the way back down to the hamlet of Horner.

There is the prospect of spotting grey wagtails and even the elusive dipper, a small bird which feeds along the rocky bottom of the river.

10. After passing over a packhorse bridge, you reach the metalled road. Horner Vale Tea Gardens are immediately before you and just to the right are the Horner Tea Gardens. A footpath leads around the end of these tea gardens into the car park.

After the walk, just a short drive will take you to the tiny hamlet of Stoke Pero where the small and robust church, at 309m above sea level, is the highest on Exmoor.

Walk 2
SELWORTHY AND BOSSINGTON

The west of Somerset is wonderful walking country and the area covered in this delightful circuit is no exception. Be sure to take your camera, for en route you will pass through 'chocolate box' villages and picture postcard scenery that must be amongst the most photographed in the country, including spectacular views across Porlock Bay, wooded valleys and open moorland. Starting in either Allerford or Bossington, the route offers a choice of three delightful teashops, one in perhaps the most picturesque setting anywhere in the country. There is a steep climb up from near Hurlstone Point to Bossington Hill but the effort is rewarded with magnificent views.

Selworthy's Periwinkle Cottage Tea Rooms, about a mile from the end of the walk, are in the vehicle-free, idyllic setting of the village green, around which are placed delightful thatched cottages. As well as delicious home-made cakes and their famous cream teas, various ploughman's lunches, salads and sandwiches are served. Inside seating is available plus space for 40 or so visitors in the gardens. The last time I was there I had the treat of watching a cock pheasant stroll over the grass and beneath my table. This was quite foolish on the part of the pheasant since my border collie was resting at my feet! The hours are 10.30 am to 5 pm and the tea rooms are open from Easter to mid-September for seven days a week, and in March and October for six days a week excluding Mondays. Telephone: 01643 862769.

The gardens of the village post office at Allerford provide an alternative venue for tea in summer (telephone: 01643 862410), and in Bossington, next to the car park, will be found Kitnor's Tea Rooms and Garden (telephone: 01643 862643). The unusual name comes from William de Ketnor, a onetime Norman landowner in the area. The tea rooms are set in a delightful thatched cottage where home-made cakes and a range of hot and cold sweet and savoury dishes are served all day, between mid-March and October, from 10.30 am to 5 pm except Wednesday and Thursday.

For the winter months, the Wortleberry Tea Room can be found in the High Street of nearby Porlock, about 1½ miles from the car park at the starting point. It is open all year, dogs are welcomed in the walled patio, and their scones come well recommended. Telephone: 01643 862337.

DISTANCE: 6½ miles.
MAP: OS Outdoor Leisure 9 Exmoor.
STARTING POINT: The free car park at Allerford (GR 904469).
HOW TO GET THERE: The village of Allerford is signposted off the A39 between Minehead and Porlock. Shortly after leaving the A39, the car park can be found on your left-hand side.
ALTERNATIVE STARTING POINT: The free car park at Bossington. This is easy to spot in the centre of the village close to Kitnor's Tea Rooms and with a red phone box at its entrance. The walk would then start at point 3.

THE WALK

1. From the car park, turn left onto the road, continue past the post office (with its tea gardens in season) and turn right at the far end of the village along a drive, signposted 'Stotes Farm and Bossington 1 mile'.

2. Cross the footbridge and follow the lower path to keep the stream on your left-hand side. In a while, the stream turns away from you and you bear uphill into the woods. On arriving at the junction of four paths, take the lower one to the left, signposted to Bossington. Continue through two stiles along the well-defined path.

Just after crossing a small stream, go through a field gate signposted 'Bossington'. Walk through the field and on the far side pass through a gate and turn left, again signposted to Bossington.

At the kissing gate and T-junction, turn left and cross over the footbridge into the car park (with public toilets) at Bossington.

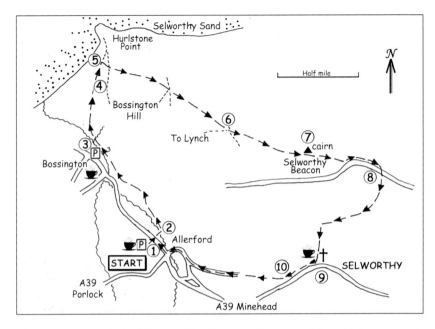

Here you can visit the Kitnor's Tea Rooms, if you so wish, which can easily be spotted at the exit from the car park. Bossington, which has attractive thatched cottages and a beach that is just ½ mile from the village, is an excellent centre for walking.

3. Retrace your steps over the footbridge and turn left, signposted to Hurlstone. Keeping the stream on your left, follow the path as it curves right uphill and away from the stream and then along the edge of woodland.

Here you will have fine views along Bossington Beach to your left and to Bossington Hill to your right.

4. When the path forks and you are faced with a choice of two gates (GR: 898487). Take the one on the right leading uphill onto open moorland.

5. You will come to a National Trust cairn near a small wooden bench.

This is an excellent spot to sit and rest, admiring the views of nearby Hurlstone Point, and across Porlock Bay to Porlock and beyond that the north coast of Devon. But don't be in a rush to leave this idyllic spot, for the next stretch is somewhat strenuous but again you will be rewarded with magnificent views.

From the cairn, follow the uphill path, signposted to Minehead. A long hard climb brings you to the top of the combe. Here the coast path goes off to the left but you need to go straight ahead, climbing towards Selworthy Beacon. On reaching a crossing of paths, continue straight on, signposted 'Coast Path Minehead'. As you progress ever upwards, a path merges from your left and later the bridleway to Lynch merges from your right. But you just keep going straight on and now slightly uphill.

6. Shortly after, the dirt road forks and you take the left-hand path. Paths merge from left and right but just keep straight along the obvious track and you will reach Selworthy Beacon with its cairn.

7. Continue along the same road past the beacon and on to join the metalled road. Turn left.

8. Shortly after rounding a right-hand bend, turn right onto a footpath signposted to Selworthy and Dunster. Very soon bear right at the T-junction, again signposted to Selworthy and Dunster. At a crossing of paths, turn right, signposted 'Selworthy', heading down into a wooded valley.

9. Continue to the end of the lane to emerge through a gate alongside Selworthy church onto the metalled road. Almost immediately turn right again through another gate to enter the higher end of the village green.

The 14th-century church is unusually a brilliant white colour and hence is something of a landmark. It is well worth a visit for the view across to Dunkery from its south porch. In contrast, the village green with its scattered thatched cottages is like a secret, hidden world. Surprisingly, as they look much older, they were built in the 19th century by the Acland family for their estate workers and retired employees.

Leave the village green from the lower end and emerge onto the metalled road. Turn right here and continue to the bottom of the village.

10. Turn right where it is signposted 'Allerford 1 mile' and pass through Selworthy Farm to enter a hedge-lined track. When the path forks, take the lower path, signposted 'Allerford ½ mile'. Follow the path to where it joins the metalled road and go straight on, signposted 'Allerford ¼ mile'. The road soon bears left and drops down to an old clapper bridge and the village of Allerford. You will now be able to see the car park to your right.

Walk 3
TARR STEPS

This undulating walk, high on Exmoor, offers magnificent scenery from fast flowing rivers to the open moorland. Although the Tarr Farm Inn is chosen as the prime tea garden for this walk, an alternative is Parsonage Farm, a little further along the route, which is in a glorious setting and a visit will be rewarded with a most friendly welcome. I like to make a day of this walk, taking lunch at Parsonage Farm and then a cream tea at Tarr Farm Inn. The route starts and finishes at the car park at Tarr Steps, the finest clapper bridge in England, which crosses the 55 ft wide river in 17 spans of flat stones.

The Tarr Farm Inn dates back to the 16th century and tastefully combines pub and tea gardens. Set high on a bank overlooking the ancient Tarr Steps, ample seating can be found both inside and out. Cream teas, cakes, gateaux, ploughman's lunches, speciality teas, soup, sandwiches and a variety of hot meals are offered during the day. The tea gardens are open all year from 11 am to 5.30 pm, and the inn reopens later for dinner, with a full à la carte menu. Telephone: 01643 851507.

At Parsonage Farm, through which the walk passes, you will find sandwiches, ploughman's, salads, soups, cream teas and basically anything that's available at the time. The scrambled eggs are famous! This is an isolated working hill farm where a fine herd of the rare Gloucester cattle is being built up, and the teashop is open all year round. The view from the gardens is wonderful, looking down over a valley, and there is alternative space inside. Telephone: 01643 831503.

DISTANCE: 7 miles.

MAP: Outdoor Leisure 9 Exmoor.

STARTING POINT: The car park up the hill from Tarr Steps (GR 872324).

HOW TO GET THERE: Take the B3223, which runs between Simonsbath and Dulverton. About 5 miles north of Dulverton, turn off the B3223 to head west following the tourist signposts for Tarr Steps. Pass through the hamlet of Liscombe and continue to follow the signs for Tarr Steps. As you descend a hill, there is a large car park on your left.

ALTERNATIVE STARTING POINT: Another possibility is to start the walk at Anstey Gate (point 10), where there is ample off road parking.

THE WALK

☕ **1.** Leave the car park at the bottom end and follow the footpath down to where Tarr Steps cross the river. Go over the clapper bridge.

2. Avoid the footpath to the right, which follows the river. Instead, immediately after, where the road forks, go right and sharp uphill, signposted to Withypool and Hawkridge. In 80 yards, fork right (waymarked in blue) to avoid the hotel and follow the steep stony track uphill, ignoring the gates to left and right.

3. Pass through a gate and follow the sunken track, which bears to the right. Continue to a gate but bear left just before it, as indicated by a blue arrow, keeping the field boundary on your right hand side. Continue until a field gate appears before you. Pass through this and keep in the same direction but now with the field boundary on your left. Pass through another gate and field in the same fashion, again following the blue arrow. At the next gate continue downhill, signposted as a footpath to Hawkridge.

☕ **4.** This path leads you into Parsonage Farm. If not stopping for refreshments, pass through the farm complex, keeping the farmhouse on

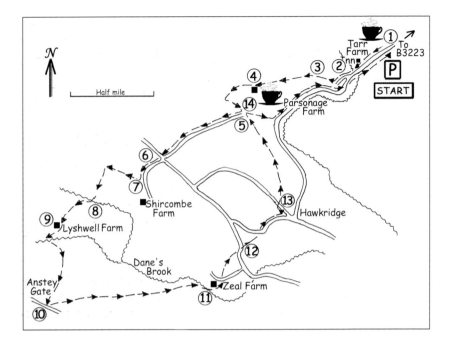

your left, and follow the track downhill and then up to where it meets the bottom end of a metalled road.

5. Turn right here onto the road and follow this up to Tarr Post on the Withypool road.

6. Turn left at Tarr Post and in 40 yards turn right onto a track to Shircombe Farm. Follow the track down to where it bends to the left.

7. At the bend, enter the field to the right. As you stand at the gate to this field, another gate can be seen in the hedge on the lower side of the field over to your left. Head for this gate and, once through it, turn right to follow the field boundary, keeping it on your right-hand side. Follow this around two sides of the field until in the bottom corner, often dense with bracken, you will find a footpath sign with the yellow end pointing to Anstey Gate, your direction. At the bottom end of the field, just after a farm track crosses your path, cross over Dane's Brook using the wooden footbridge.

8. Immediately after the bridge, turn right to walk a few yards upstream on the left-hand bank to where a tree-lined gullied path leads uphill. The

The ancient stone clapper bridge at Tarr Steps

gulley peters out as a low bank appears. Follow this uphill and then bear right as you approach the field boundary to go through a gate, after which you bear left to follow the yellow markers, passing the farm on its left.

9. Turn right after the generator building (which you can probably hear chugging away inside), and follow the farm road through the gate and all the way up to Anstey Gate where you emerge by a large stony car parking area.

10. Pass through the gate to your left and follow the track that goes off diagonally to your left, away from the road, signposted in blue as the footpath to Hawkridge. The track leads gently downhill and then, once you have passed over at least half the length of the common, it levels off just as you reach a stand of gorse bushes. The way forks just after the bushes and you need to take the path dropping downhill to the left, passing just to the left of the next stand of gorse bushes, but continuing in the same direction. In the distance before you can be seen a meadow at the bottom end of the valley between the moorland to the right and woods to the left. This acts as a marker for your general direction, which is important since the path becomes less distinct in places, fading away and then returning several times, eventually becoming more gullied as it drops down to Dane's Brook. Just keep heading towards that meadow in the distance. On reaching the brook, use the stepping stones to cross the river.

There will be occasions when there is too much water in the brook to cross it safely on the stones. In such cases, follow the bank downstream to cross at Slade Bridge. Go over the bridge and follow the road up to the entrance to Zeal Farm. Continue uphill and just where the road bears sharp right and then left, you rejoin the proper route at point 12.

11. Pass through the gate and follow the track up to Zeal Farm. Go through an iron gate and in a few yards a white gate. Turn right here to follow the farm track towards the road. Just before the last farm buildings on your left-hand side, turn left to cross the open field diagonally to a gate in the top corner. Pass through this gate and cross the next field by heading towards the short stretch of metalled road that can be seen slightly to your left. This leads you to the top corner of the field to a small wooden gate which you won't see until you're closer. After the gate, cross the road to the two field gates on the opposite side.

12. Take the furthest of the two gates and follow the route signposted 'Hawkridge', bearing half left across the field to reach a gate in the top left corner of the field, just before the house whose rooftop can be seen in front of you. Pass through the gate and turn right onto the metalled road into the village of Hawkridge. Turn left at the phone box, signposted 'Withypool', and then right immediately after the letterbox onto a footpath signposted to Tarr Steps, and follow the yellow markers.

13. After passing through the initial gate and stile, cross the field diagonally to your left to the field gate with a yellow marker just to the right of a telegraph pole that is also marked with yellow. In the next field go diagonally right to the field gate with a yellow marker. Beyond that gate, keep in the same general direction, following the right hand field boundary to the next waymarked gate. After that gate, avoid the path that leads uphill to the left. Just continue in the same direction, keeping the dense woodland to your right. The path leads you on through two more fields, with the woodland on your right, until you reach a gate that takes you out onto a metalled road.

14. You have been here already – this is point 5 on the map. Turn right here, signposted 'Tarr Steps' and head downhill. At the metalled road, turn left and follow the road back to Tarr Steps, Tarr Farm Inn and the car park.

Walk 4
DULVERTON AND THE RIVER BARLE

This delightful walk follows the River Barle whose fast-flowing waters run through the Exmoor village of Dulverton. Just one moderate uphill section marks the midpoint of the route, otherwise it's easy going with well-defined paths. The Heritage Centre, which you pass on your way back, is well worth a visit, as is the Exmoor National Park Information Centre, which borders the car park where the circuit starts and finishes. There are also some excellent shops to browse, with guns, fishing tackle and country-wear indicating the importance of Dulverton as a centre for the Exmoor community.

Dulverton is well blessed with teashops. The one I have chosen is Lewis's Tearooms, situated at 13 High Street, just up from the river bridge. Offering some exceptional fare in a spacious setting, the building dates back over 200 years. A wide selection of food is served including such delights as Somerset rarebit topped with cider cream and local Brie. Indeed there is a whole range of rarebits and the specials change by the day. At teatime the carrot cake is very popular and, of course, cream teas are available. Walkers are especially welcome, as are dogs. Lewis's is open all year (except for one or two weeks in January for maintenance) from 10 am to 5 pm. Telephone: 01398 323850.

Alternatively, just along the road, at 21 Fore Street, there are the excellent Copper Kettle Tea Rooms, which nestle beneath a heavily wooded hillside. The tables inside cater for around 30 customers whilst there is ample additional seating in the gardens to the rear. The menu offers a range of salads, ploughman's, cakes and cream teas, also home-made soup 'to die for', as I was told by two fellow walkers I met on Selworthy Beacon. The tea rooms are open all year round, 10.30 am to 5 pm on weekdays and 12 noon to 5 pm on Sundays (closed at Christmas and some Sundays during the winter months). Telephone: 01398 323697.

DISTANCE: 3½ miles.
MAP: OS Outdoor Leisure 9 Exmoor.
STARTING POINT: The car park (pay and display) by the bridge crossing the River Barle in the village centre (GR 912279).
HOW TO GET THERE: From Minehead/Dunster, take the A396 south through Dunster and in about 14 miles turn right, signposted to Dulverton. From Tiverton take the A396 north and turn left, again signposted to Dulverton. In the village centre, all roads lead downhill to where the main road crosses the River Barle. A well signposted car park will be found behind the Bridge Inn and adjacent to the Exmoor Park headquarters. A statue of Lorna Doone marks the entrance to the park. Alternative parking can be found in the Guildhall car park (pay and display), which adjoins the riverside car park via a small wooden bridge and is signposted from the main street.

The Walk

1. From the car park, return to the five-arched bridge and turn right to cross the River Barle. Turn immediately right again and, just after Rose Cottage, take the signposted footpath with a notice pointing to Horner Cottage.

2. At Horner Cottage, take the path to the right, signposted to Tarr Steps. Ignore the 'Middle Path' signposted to your left. Your path leads you on until it rejoins the river with a white house opposite with a fording track alongside it. Just continue from here along the same path, with the river on your right, to ascend a short steep incline. There is a welcoming bench

22

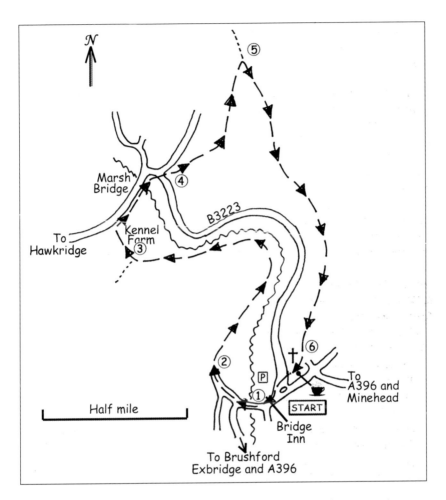

at the crest. Just after a chicane stile barrier (to prevent horses and motor bikes), the path forks.

In this section of the walk, you are passing through Burridge Wood, which was gifted for public use by two local worthies. High up through the trees will be found the remnants of the earth banks of Oldberry Castle, the remains of an Iron Age hill fort. Across the other side of the valley, the hillside rises with nearly vertical cliffs giving quite splendid views in contrast to the low-lying meadowland in between. During the early summer months, there is a strong smell of wild garlic along here and later the rhododendrons take control.

3. Keep to the right-hand path, signposted 'Marsh Bridge'. In about 100 yards the path leads you through Kennel Farm and onto the metalled road. Turn right here and in 300 yards cross Marsh Bridge.

A field gate provides your way through the farmyard. Please be careful to ensure the gate is closed behind you.

4. On crossing the bridge, turn immediately right and go over a small stone bridge. The road forks immediately in front of you. Take the left fork and in 20 yards cross the road* to follow an uphill track signposted as a 'RUPP', a road used as a public path, to Court Down and Northcombe. Follow this (ignoring a path which merges quite early from your right) all the way to the very top.

* Please cross with caution – listen for traffic coming down the hill from your left and appearing rapidly round the sharp bend.
The mix of woodland and meadow along this uphill section provides some excellent birdsong during the spring months. On the higher part of the path, watch out for hares, which I have seen along here on several occasions.

5. At the top of the track, turn right signposted 'Dulverton'. From here, your path couldn't be easier. The route is obvious all the way and gradually descends into Dulverton village centre.

On reaching a school warning sign, step to the left to look at the rooftops of the village from the field gate. It's a magnificent view and makes one realise how lucky the village children were to have such a setting, except of course in the snow and ice covered months of late winter.

6. Turn left at the old school and almost immediately turn right, down steps which lead you past the church, and continue downhill past the Lion Inn and the post office, heading downhill towards the river and your car park. You will find the Copper Kettle Tea Rooms on your right-hand side and shortly after, Lewis's Tearooms.

Across the road can be found the unusually designed Town Hall with its double-sided arched staircase. After the Tourist Information Office, you can turn right to find the village Heritage Centre, which is well worth a visit. This also provides an alternative and shorter route back to your car park. After passing the Heritage Centre, continue on into the Guildhall car park from where a pedestrian exit leads into the riverside car park.

Walk 5
DUNSTER

The walk starts from the village, or strictly speaking town, of Dunster with its fairy-tale castle. It is ideal for a hot summer's day when the shelter of the trees, for almost the complete circuit, provides welcome shade. The route, albeit over hills, has a predominantly easy gradient – what steep bits there are prove to be fairly short – and incorporates a visit to an Iron Age fort whose title of Bat's Castle conjures up images of Dracula, whilst the next hill along takes its name from the gallows which are reputed to have been sited there. Despite that, it really is a very pleasant walk!

 Dunster can claim an abundance of teashops, all of them offering good food with good service. However, most of them front onto the main road through the village, which is fine if you wish to watch the traffic go by. In contrast, the Dunster Mill Tea Rooms and Gardens in Mill Lane are set idyllically alongside the river next to the historically important mill where stone ground flour is still produced and on sale. The owners specialise in home baking, and everything is home-made. Light lunches are available and the cream teas are considered by many to be served with the best scones in Somerset. Meals can be taken alongside the river in the garden setting or under cover in the tea rooms. Opening times are 10.30 am to 4.45 pm from 1st April to 31st October. Closed on Fridays except in July and August. Telephone: 01643 821759.

When the Dunster Mill Tea Rooms are closed, there are several alternatives within a short walking distance, many of them open all year round.

DISTANCE: 4½ miles.
MAP: OS Outdoor Leisure 9 Exmoor.
STARTING POINT: The car park by the Gallox Bridge in Dunster (GR 989432).
HOW TO GET THERE: Dunster can be found just off the A39 between Williton and Minehead. From the A39, take the A396 into and through the village (notice the large pay and display car park on your left which is an alternative should the car park you require be full). You will pass the yarn market in the centre of the village and after driving through a series of traffic lights (the streets are very narrow here) turn left immediately after the Foresters Arms. This short lane leads you down to a pay and display car park by the packhorse bridge.

THE WALK

Dunster is one of Somerset's hot spots for tourists with its medieval streets, mill and yarn market, not to mention its wonderful castle, which stands proud over the town. Its wealth was at one time based on the wool trade and the word Dunster was synonymous with high quality woollen products. The town can still boast many excellent shops selling woollen goods.

1. From the car park, turn left to cross the Gallox Bridge and go straight ahead, keeping the two cottages on your right-hand side.

The Gallox Bridge takes its name from the Gallax Hill, which rises up from the river before you. It is one of the few remaining Exmoor ancient packhorse bridges and survives as an excellent example. Strings of ponies, with their huge loads, were once the only practical way of transporting goods in these hilly settlements.

2. Just after the cottages, take the second path on the right, which is

26

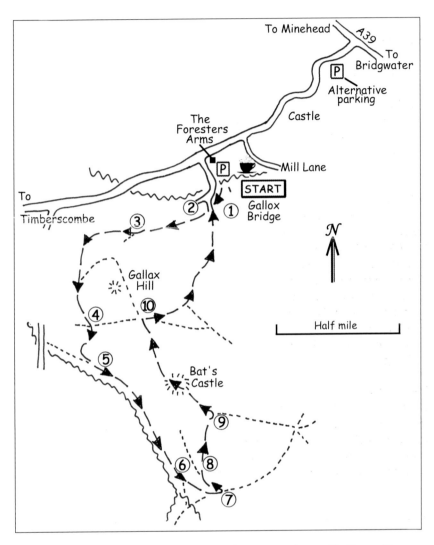

signposted 'Timberscombe, Luxborough via Croydon Hill'. You will now be entering the Dunster Woodland owned by the Crown Estates and you will climb steadily uphill.

3. When the main track appears to bear left through a gateway, ignore this and continue straight on to the right of the gate. Likewise ignore the lesser path, which later drops down to your right, by continuing uphill. Shortly after, your path will bear at a right angle to the left. At the next

The Gallox clapper bridge at Dunster (the author's dog has just spotted a red deer)

T-junction of paths, go left. Your path will now descend slowly towards the valley bottom, which you will see on your right-hand side.

In May and June this section of the walk is resplendent with rhododendrons in bloom.

4. At a crossroads of paths, just after a gate to your left, continue straight on, going slightly uphill, ignoring the path to your left going more steeply uphill and the one to your right going downhill. You will gradually drop downhill whilst the valley bottom to your right rises to meet you when your path merges with one from the right.

5. Continue forward, following the valley upstream with the sound of the stream to your right. You will pass a small but very noticeable gated quarry on your left. Eventually, at a point where a small bench built from logs sits alongside a wooden bridge leading into a meadow, the path to follow bears left and uphill away from the stream.

6. In 100 yards, the path forks with red and blue arrows pointing to the right. Take the left path, which goes relatively steeply uphill and is signposted as a 'RUPP', a road used as a public path.

7. In about 300 yards, turn sharp left where you see, close to ground level, two Crown Estate waymark posts, numbered 2 and 3. In turning left you double back on yourself in the direction indicated by the two markers.

8. In another 100 yards, turn right through a gateway (signposted 'Crown Estates 2 and 3') into coniferous woodland, following the obvious path between the trees. Continue up to the open moorland ahead.

9. Approaching the ridge, the path bears right before emerging onto the hilltop where the sea comes into view. Here you join the path that comes up on your right from Withycombe Hill Gate. Turn left onto this path (signposted 'Crown Estates 2 and 3'), heading for Bat's Castle.

Here you will enjoy fine views across Exmoor, south Wales and Conygar Hill, on which are the remains of a folly. Bat's Castle is an Iron Age fort that is still clearly visible at this summit point. The lines of the raised wall and surrounding ditch are still obvious and one can imagine just how defendable the position would have been centuries ago when the ditch would have been perhaps a metre deeper and the bank a metre higher.

The path continues through and beyond Bat's Castle towards Gallax Hill. Shortly after Bat's Castle there is a 3-seater bench – an ideal spot to take a break.

10. On reaching the bottom of the dip between Bat's Castle and Gallax Hill, turn right to descend back into the trees.

☕ In a short distance the path splits and you need to take the lesser path to the left. Ignore the path that later joins from your right and just continue downhill. Shortly after passing through a gate, bear left and then almost immediately right, past the cottages and back to the Gallox Bridge and your car park. To find the Dunster Mill Tea Rooms, leave the car park on foot and turn immediately right along the footpath between a short series of bungalows. Turn right at the other end of this path and the tea rooms will be in front of you.

Walk 6
KILVE

*T*his easy and mostly flat 3 mile walk takes in a stretch of the Somerset coastline as well as the picturesque villages of Kilve and East Quantoxhead. There is one short stretch of main road walking but the scenery and rural atmosphere of the two villages more than compensate. The chosen tea gardens are directly on the route and sit alongside an old ruined chantry where smugglers once stored their secret hoards. Coleridge and Wordsworth were regular visitors here, the latter referring to 'Kilve's delightful shore' whilst Southey also came and noted 'Kilve's green sea'.

The Chantry Tea Gardens are pleasantly situated down a quiet country lane leading to the rocky beach at Kilve. Cream teas are offered as well as sandwiches, light lunches, ploughman's, cold meats, quiches and soups. Everything is home-made except the bread, which is baked locally. The teashop is open all year except at Christmas, 10 am to 5.30 pm. Telephone: 01278 741457. Groups are welcome, if booked in advance, and seating allows in excess of 50 visitors.

DISTANCE: 3 miles.

MAP: OS Explorer 140 Quantock Hills and Bridgwater.

STARTING POINT: The car park (pay and display) at the approach to Kilve Beach (GR 144443).

HOW TO GET THERE: The village of Kilve is easily found on the main A39 between Bridgwater and Minehead. Once in the village, take the lane, Sea Lane, which runs alongside the post office and is signposted 'to the beach'. At the end there is a pay and display parking area. Public conveniences can also be found here.

ALTERNATIVE STARTING POINT: There is an alternative car park (free) in the centre of the village, almost opposite the post office and conveniently on the route. You would then start the walk at point 9.

THE WALK

1. From the car park, take the signposted footpath to the shore, passing the derelict brick-built oil retort. Go through a stile and follow the tarmac path for a short distance to reach the shoreline.

This brick and cast-iron retort is all that survives of a failed attempt in the 1920s by the Shaline Company to turn Kilve into an oil-producing centre.

2. On reaching the shore, turn left and ascend the short uphill path along the clifftop to pass through a waymarked field gate. Follow the clifftop path for the full length of the field to your left. You will come to a small, dry creek around which the coastal path skirts. Here concrete steps lead down to the beach, which you may like to take in as a detour.

3. Turn left at the dry creek to head inland, with the splendid Court House standing before you to your right. In a short distance follow the signposted path (to East Quantoxhead) between two wire fences, towards the large wood.

4. After passing through two kissing gates, turn right at the T-junction of paths, signposted 'East Quantoxhead'. Follow the path with the stream on your right until reaching the metalled road.

Here you may like to explore the church, set idyllically alongside the village duckpond, with thatched and quaint cottages to complete the tranquil scene.

For a shorter route, turn left after the second kissing gate to follow the

The village duckpond at East Quantoxhead

signposted footpath back to Kilve church. At the church, turn left to return to your car park.

5. For the main walk, turn left onto the road. Ignore the road that forks to the right and the lane that goes off to the left. Follow the road for ½ mile passing a public phone and then a letterbox on your right.

6. Immediately after a house on the left called Dreamend, turn left onto the footpath signposted to Kilve. Keeping the cottages to your left, head straight across the first field to a stile, which you cross. Turn half right to cross the field, heading towards a large dead tree. Cross the stile just to the left of the tree and walk across the next field, still following the footpath. Go over the next stile and once again head straight across the field towards a house. Just before the house, exit the field onto the road.

7. Turn left. Caution – for a short distance there is no footpath.

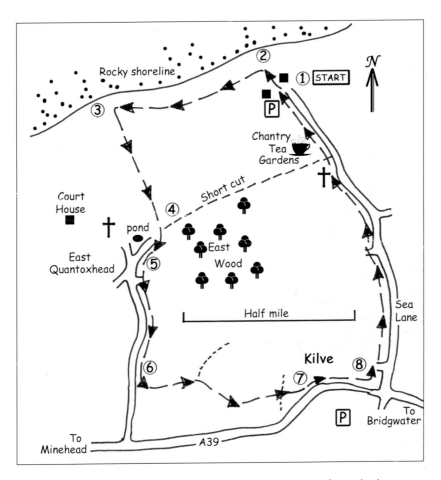

8. In a short distance you will pass the Hood Arms, after which comes the post office. Turn left here into Sea Lane and follow it to its end where you will find the car park. Partway along, on the left, you come to the Chantry Tea Gardens.

Next to the tea gardens are the ruins of an old chantry. This was used as a storage depot for smugglers. However, in 1848, when the customs men got too close for comfort, the smugglers set fire to the brandy, which blew up, leaving the priory building in ruins.

Walk 7
HOLFORD

On the section of the Quantock Hills that forms a large curving sweep where the north face is carved with the deep-sided combes visited by the poets Coleridge and Wordsworth during their sojourns in Somerset and much loved by them, the fast-flowing streams of Holford Combe and Hodder's Combe blend as one as they meet in the village of Holford. This walk takes us high up over those combes to an ancient Iron Age settlement site with spectacular views across the Bristol Channel. Since the route is mostly over high ground, it provides easy walking even after rain.

Stella's Tea Gardens – a favourite spot of mine – are at the entrance to Hodder's Combe and parking can be found a matter of yards away alongside the village green. The elm-clad tea rooms have a garden area set alongside a stream. Squirrels are regular visitors and red deer are occasionally sighted from the gardens. Hikers and bikers, muddy or immaculate, all receive a warm and friendly greeting. Both hot and cold meals are served and always with a choice of fresh seasonal vegetables and salads. The menu is unfailingly interesting with such unusual items as National Trust pie, rhubarb and honey cake, apple and sultana crumble and a whole range of expected and unexpected fare marked up on the chalkboard. Everything is home-cooked and it's never the same two weeks running. During British summer time, Stella's is open on Wednesday to Sunday plus Bank Holiday Mondays from 11 am to 6 pm; 11.30 am to 4 pm for the rest of the year. Closed on December 25th/26th. Telephone: 01278 741529.

DISTANCE: 4½ miles.
MAP: OS Explorer 140 Quantock Hills and Bridgwater.
STARTING POINT: The free car park at Holford village green (GR 154411).
HOW TO GET THERE: Holford village can be found on the A39 between Bridgwater and Minehead. From Minehead, take the second turning right once in the village. From Bridgwater, take the first left once in the village. Drive past the church, bearing left when a narrow road merges from your right. Bear right at the fork signposted for Hodder's Combe and turn left into the car park when the village green comes into view. Stella's Tea Gardens are just a few yards up the track leading into Hodder's Combe.
ALTERNATIVE STARTING POINTS: Should the car park be full, you may find it easier to leave your car in the lay-by on the main A39 road (point 2). Otherwise you could park at Dead Woman's Ditch (point 6), making the tea gardens your halfway stop.

THE WALK

1. From the car park, turn right and walk just around the corner where you bear left as you face the row of thatched cottages and then turn right at the road junction. In a matter of yards, turn left onto a narrow road, which goes uphill quite steeply to the left. Whistlers Cottage will be on your left. Follow this road over the small hill to just before the lay-by on the A39 where you will see a National Trust sign for Woodlands Hill on the right hand side at the gated entrance to the woods (GR 155407).

2. Take the path by that sign through the gate into the woods, following the distinct path that winds up Woodlands Hill with woods on your left and open fields and then moorland on your right. As you come out of the woods, the path forks in front of you. Take the path on the right, which continues uphill and away from the trees.

3. You will come to an 8 ft high cairn at 846 ft above sea level (GR 156399). The hilltop of Dowsborough is now before you and the path to the top is clearly visible. Before you reach Dowsborough, a path crosses from left to right in front of you. A wooden signpost tries to direct you to the left. Ignore this and head straight on to the summit.

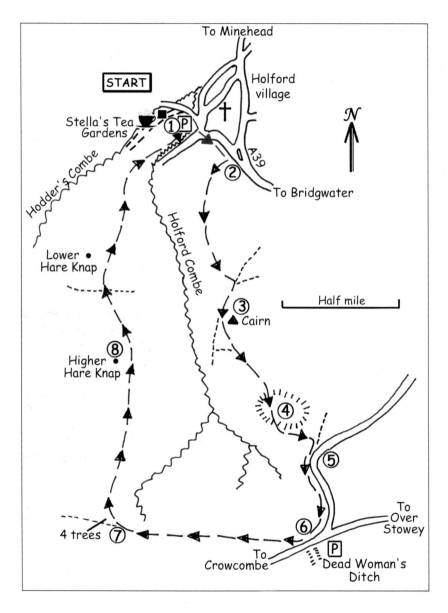

4. As you enter Dowsborough at the summit, you will notice the embankment that goes all the way around this old Iron Age fortress. Inside the walled area the summit is covered in a thicket and a path runs around the outside of the thicket and just inside the embankment.

Locally Dowsborough is called Danesborough. It was an Iron Age hill fort from around 700 BC to the time of the Roman invasion. As you enter the fort, the first distinguishing feature is the ditch followed by the raised bank and in places, there is still a difference of 12 ft in height.

Follow the path to the right which takes you anticlockwise around the inside of the old fort, bearing left all the time until you reach a gap in the embankment where the path splits. The left hand path continues inside the wall but you need the path to the right. It crosses the bank and the ditch to take you gently downhill to a T-junction where you turn right and then in a short distance you emerge onto a narrow and quiet metalled road (GR 161387).

5. Turn right here and head uphill to a point where another narrow metalled road merges from your left-hand side. You will find a parking area at a spot known as Dead Woman's Ditch where the shape of another old embankment can be seen running off to the left.

This ditch was the site of first burial place of Jane Shorney, murdered in 1789 by her husband John Walford, a charcoal burner. Evidence of coppiced woodlands from those days still abound. He was hanged just down the road at a place now called Walford's Gibbet.

6. Continue uphill for just a few yards to where a dirt track leads off to your right, marked with a wooden 'No Vehicles' post. Follow this well-defined track, keeping the woodland on your right and moorland on your left. Eventually you come to a point where the path forks in front of you, with a group of four trees, one with a double trunk, standing in the narrow wedge of the fork.

7. Take the right hand path here, which temporarily drops downhill, heading towards the higher ground of Higher Hare Knap. Just beyond that and to its left will be seen Lower Hare Knap.

8. Continue past Higher Hare Knap, and as you approach Lower Hare Knap the path forks (GR 150394), uphill to the left, heading to the knap, or slightly downhill to the right. Take the right-hand track, still well defined, following this all the way back to the car park.

Walk 8
TRISCOMBE

This is a 3½ mile up and down route from the village of Triscombe, taking in Will's Neck, the highest point on the Quantock Hills. There is a moderately strenuous uphill section of about ½ mile (between points 3 and 4) but after the walk it adds to the pleasure as you sit in the delightful tea rooms with panoramic views across landscaped gardens to the nearby ranges of hills.

 Stable Cottage is situated at the foot of Will's Neck at Triscombe, with wonderful views along the Quantock Hills and across to the Brendon Hills, Exmoor and the Blackdown Hills. Originally built as stables for nearby Triscombe House, the building now comprises living quarters and tea rooms, of which there are three. A large conservatory has been added and it's all set in spacious, lovingly-tended landscaped grounds. During the winter months, the Tack Room boasts an open fire.

Stable Cottage has built up an enviable reputation for its food and surroundings and is one of the most frequently mentioned teashops among the walking fraternity in this area. Cream teas, home-made cakes and a highly recommended rich fruit cake, a speciality of the house, plus a selection of teas and coffees are on offer, and local jams, cream and other produce are used wherever possible. Lucky visitors may see the wild red deer, if not in the adjoining fields, then up on the hill which slopes up to Will's Neck and which is in open view from the gardens and conservatory.

The tea rooms are open on Tuesday to Sunday, plus Bank Holiday Mondays, from Easter (or 1st April, whichever comes earliest) to the end of October, 2 pm to 5.30 pm. From November to Easter they are open just at weekends, 2 pm to 5 pm. Sunday lunches are usually available at 12.30 pm but booking is essential due to Stable Cottage's popularity. Telephone: 01984 618239.

When the tea rooms are closed, an alternative refreshment stop is the Blue Ball Inn adjacent to the car park. Hot and cold meals are served during normal licensing hours.

DISTANCE: 3½ miles.
MAP: OS Explorer 140 Quantock Hills and Bridgwater.
STARTING POINT: The car park (free) opposite the Blue Ball Inn at Triscombe (GR 155355).
HOW TO GET THERE: Stable Cottage is located just north of the A358 between Taunton and Williton. Triscombe is signposted off this road and the tea rooms are on the right-hand side. Continue along this road (for a further ½ mile) to the car park across the road from the Blue Ball Inn at Triscombe for the start of the walk.
ALTERNATIVE STARTING POINT: You could start the walk from the Triscombe Stone car park (also free) (GR 164359) – see point 6 – at the top of Cockercombe, which is approached from the other side of the hills. The Cockercombe road is accessed from the road running between Plainsfield and Over Stowey to the south of the A39 and Nether Stowey.

THE WALK

1. On leaving the car park, turn left and then immediately right to take the road that runs up behind the Blue Ball Inn, signposted to West Bagborough. The road bears left and goes uphill.

2. At the point where the road bears right and appears to go downhill, take the track to the left and continue gradually uphill. Ignore the gated

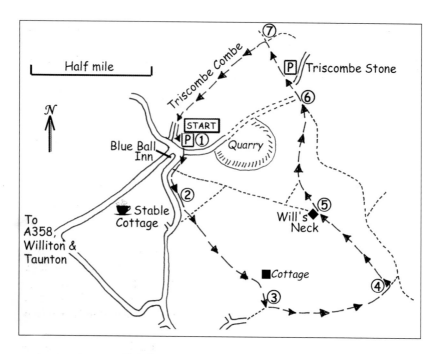

Half mile

N

To
A358,
Williton &
Taunton

Triscombe Combe

Triscombe Stone

START

Blue Ball Inn

Quarry

Stable Cottage

Will's Neck

Cottage

track that bears off left and continue along the signposted footpath, dropping gradually downhill until crossing a stream where a small white cottage can be seen to the left. Continue along the path until, dropping downhill again, you reach a gate that leads into a lane and to Rock Farm.

3. A few yards before reaching the gate, turn sharp left to head steeply back uphill. Ignore the gated lane that crosses your path and continue uphill for about ½ mile.

There are some fine sweet chestnut trees as you pass through these woods, although I have yet to find any chestnuts large enough for roasting, and lime trees on the right as you proceed higher through the woodland.

4. Just after emerging from the woods you reach the crest of the hill. Here you will find a small pond scraped out of the earth on the right-hand side by the tree line.

The pond, sometimes dry at the end of a long hot spell, provides a watering hole for the Quantock ponies which can often be seen of an evening as they ascend the hill to linger in this normally cool area. These occasional

40

damp spots on the Quantocks are often favourite gathering places for the red deer in the rutting season. The stags like to roll in the moist ground and leave their scent. When rutting, usually around October, they can be heard bellowing as they call for the attention of the hinds.

Just a few yards after this, a wide path crosses yours as it runs along the Quantock ridge. Turn left onto this ridge path. In about 100 yards, the track splits. Bear right and continue along this track until reaching the triangulation point at Will's Neck.

Will's Neck is the highest point on the Quantock Hills at 1,260 ft above sea level and offers wide views across Exmoor on one side and to the coast of south Wales on the other.

5. After the triangulation point, the path splits. Take the right-hand path, which leads downhill, gradually approaching the woods to your right. On reaching the tree line, bear left keeping to the bold path which drops downhill skirting the quarry to your left. Continue along the track to where it joins another more obvious track just after a wooden bench seat.

6. Turn left onto the main track and ignore the roads to left and right at the cattle grid.

Triscombe Stone is an ancient stone with all kinds of associated legends, mostly to do with the Devil. It is recommended therefore that this walk should only be attempted in daylight! Here you will find the car park that is the alternative parking place for your walk. If you have parked here, then your directions are to cross the cattle grid from the car park, turn right onto the tree-lined track and continue as below.

Continue straight ahead along the tree-lined path.

7. You soon reach a gate crossing the path with a National Trust property sign declaring 'Great and Marrow Hills'. Pass through the gate and turn left over the stile into a fenced common area. After crossing the stile, bear right along a track leading you along the top of the field. As you near a gate on your right-hand side, with an earth bank in front of you, turn left to follow the track as it meanders down through the valley bottom, with Marrow Hill to your left and Great Hill to your right, eventually emerging onto a road. Turn left here and in a matter of yards you arrive at the car park.

Walk 9
TAUNTON

This is an interesting 4 mile circuit from the centre of Taunton following the banks of the River Tone and the Bridgwater and Taunton Canal. It is very easy walking, being level along its entire length. Taunton is the county town of Somerset and as such is well blessed with cafés, restaurants and teashops. The chosen refreshment stop is, however, directly on the route in a riverside position, with an alternative courtyard café nearby.

The Flying Aubergine, just by the Town Bridge, is light and airy and pleasantly situated for a town centre café, overlooking the river. Seating is available inside and out. There is a range of hot and cold meals and drinks, including daily specials, and the cakes are made locally. Open every day throughout the year except at Christmas, 9 am to 5.30 pm (6 pm on Saturday). Telephone: 01823 352033.

An alternative is the Flowers Restaurant and Coffee House in St James Courtyard just off St James Street. Open every day except Sundays and bank holidays, 9 am to 5 pm, 4 pm on Wednesdays. Closed at Christmas. Telephone: 01823 324354.

DISTANCE: 4 miles.

MAP: OS Explorer 128 Taunton and Blackdown Hills.

STARTING POINT: The pay and display car park on Priory Bridge Road, opposite the cricket ground and Volvo garage (GR 232251).

HOW TO GET THERE: From the M5 at junction 25, head into Taunton. Go straight across at the two roundabouts. At the second there is a petrol station. Your road goes just to the right of it. Shortly after there is a large Volvo garage and beyond that the County Cricket Ground, both on your left. On your right, opposite these, is a large public car park, which is your start point.

ALTERNATIVE STARTING POINT: An alternative is to use the St James Street car park (also pay and display) by following the signs for the Brewhouse Theatre. At the petrol station referred to earlier, bear left instead of right. The theatre is conveniently alongside your walk and is in fact closer to the two recommended tea rooms. However, the parking there is busier and spaces can be hard to find on busy days. You would then start the walk at point 2.

THE WALK

☕ **1.** On the far side of the car park turn left at the path to follow the riverside walk with the River Tone on your right-hand side. You will go under a bridge and then pass the cricket ground and Brewhouse Theatre on your left. Just after the theatre, as you approach the ornate Town Bridge, you reach the Flying Aubergine on your left-hand side.

Standing at the front of the café and looking down through a side street, you can see a Wimpy burger house. If you head for this, turn left and then right into St James Courtyard, you will find the alternative choice of the Flowers Restaurant and Coffee House.

2. At the bridge, turn left to use the light-controlled crossing over the road. Immediately in front of you is a gap between two buildings (with Debenhams on your left), which takes you into Goodland Gardens. Continue to follow the riverbank. After crossing a small arched bridge over a side stream, turn right over the footbridge to cross the River Tone.

3. Once across the bridge, turn left to follow the riverbank, now on your left-hand side. On reaching a short stretch of roadway, keep following the river into a park. Follow the path until reaching a weir.

4. Do not cross the bridge at the weir but keep straight ahead to follow the park boundary still with the river on your left. On leaving the park,

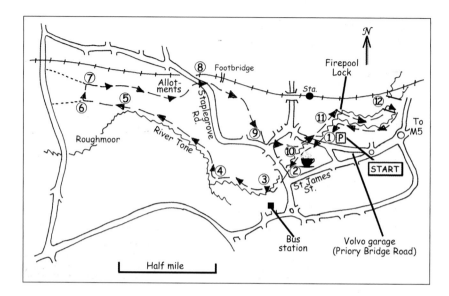

turn left to enter a path signposted as 'Two Counties Way'. Your path continues with the river to your left and housing to your right.

5. Follow this well-worn path until eventually it leads away from the river towards whitewashed houses.

6. Just before the first white house, turn right onto a signposted footpath between two lengths of fence.

7. In about 160 yards, cross a stile to enter a large field where you immediately turn right to follow the right-hand field boundary back towards Taunton. At the end of the field, continue straight ahead into the next field. The path soon passes through allotments, then along the backs of houses, finally along the front of a row of cottages before emerging onto Staplegrove Road.

8. Cross this road and continue opposite into Chip Lane. Walk down the right-hand side and, at the end of the road, continue straight ahead in the same direction, past the black railway footbridge. Still walking in the same direction, follow the footpath, with a high wall on the right.

9. Continue all the way to the end of the footpath, where it emerges once again onto Staplegrove Road. Turn left and in a short distance the road

Taunton's attractive Town Bridge

splits. Here you bear slightly left (in the direction of the railway station) and cross the road using the pedestrian crossing. Once across, turn left and almost immediately right into the gap between two shops. At the end of this very short lane, turn right and then left to go through the Safeway supermarket 'Welcome' archway. Walk straight ahead along the front of the supermarket to the far end of the building. In front of you will be seen the roof shelters protecting some walkways beyond a red brick wall. Use the steps here to cross the wall.

10. Turn left at the riverbank and follow the riverside walk with the river on your right. Pass under the first bridge and continue past the second.

11. In a short distance you reach the Firepool Lock where the canal joins the River Tone. Turn right (signposted 'National Cycle Network 3 – Bridgwater and Creech St Michael') to cross the canal bridge. After going over the bridge, turn left to follow the canal path with the canal on your left.

12. At the next bridge, take the path up to the right of the bridge and turn right at the top. Cross over the next bridge (River Tone) and then turn right to follow the riverside path back to your car park.

Walk 10
BURNHAM-ON-SEA

This varied route takes in an old Roman encampment, two lighthouses and a stretch of beach. Wonderful views across the countryside open up on the top of Brent Knoll. It is an easy walk, being mostly flat with just the climb to the Knoll halfway around.

French's Café Bar in Burnham-on-Sea is a light and airy establishment in College Street, a side street running up from the sea front. Seating is available both inside and outside on the enclosed pavement area. There is a range of drinks and hot and cold meals including omelettes, sandwiches, baguettes, quiches, jackets and daily specials, also home-made cakes. Open every day throughout the year including Christmas Day, 9 am to 11 pm on Monday to Saturday and 10 am to 3 pm on Sunday. Telephone: 01278 788415.

DISTANCE: 7½ miles.
MAP: OS Explorer 153 Weston-Super-Mare and Bleadon Hill.
STARTING POINT: French's Café Bar in College Street (GR 304492).
HOW TO GET THERE: Burnham is easily accessed from the A38 or junction 22 of

the M5. Follow the signs to the sea front, looking for a convenient roadside parking spot in or near the town centre. College Street is a side street running off from the sea front immediately opposite the pier. French's Café Bar will be found between the High Street and Oxford Street on the left hand side as you travel away from the coast. Alternatively, you could use the long stay car park (fee payable) next to the supermarket on the sea front opposite the tourist information office, to the south of the pier. From here, to find the French's Café Bar simply walk along to the pier and turn right into College Street.

THE WALK

1. From French's Café Bar, walk away from the sea to reach Oxford Street. Turn left and at the roundabout, turn right into Love Lane. Continue along this busy road, going straight across at the next roundabout, until just as you approach a large sign thanking you for visiting Burnham-on-Sea, you leave the road by turning left onto a signposted footpath.

2. Enter the field and, ignoring the tempting gap in the hedge on the right, continue in the direction as indicated by the signpost. Find the gap in the hedge at the end of the path and cross a ditch over a railway sleeper bridge. Turn slightly left to pass through a grey metal gate. After this, turn right and keep the field boundary ditch on your right, heading for the railway line before you.

3. Cross the railway line at the pedestrian crossing to enter the caravan park.

Cross the line with caution. High speed trains use the line but there is good visibility for a long distance in both directions.

Turn left between the two stiles to skirt along the edge of the park through a tree-lined bower. In about 100 yards, turn right through a gate and then turn right at the tarmac road to head through the caravan park to the main entrance gates. There is ample signage to indicate your way to the exit. Leaving the site, turn left onto the road and in a short distance turn right by the whitewashed corrugated metal chapel into a lane.

4. About 150 yards along the lane, turn right onto a footpath between two houses.

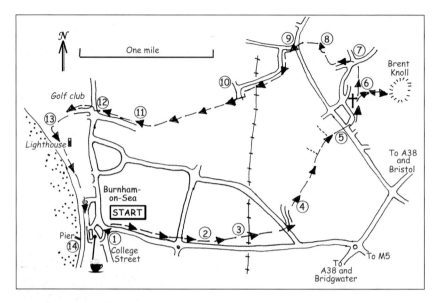

This can be difficult to spot. The entrance can be somewhat overgrown and is found between two posts. If you reach the farm, you have overshot. There is a sign stating 'Footpath' which is most easily seen looking back once you've passed it.

Cross a railway sleeper footbridge to enter a field. Bear left and follow the left-hand field boundary, ignoring a gate and footbridge to your left, until you reach the top corner of the field where you pass through a gate into a green lane. At the end of the lane, enter the left of the two fields. Looking across the field towards the church, you will see a field gate in the hedge. About 70 yards to the left of this there is a railway sleeper bridge crossing the ditch. Head for this and cross into the next field.

If the bridge is overgrown with brambles, use the field gate.

Bear slightly left and head for the next field gate. Pass through the gate and go straight ahead. At the end of the lane there is a choice of three fields. Cross the stile into the one on your right, turn left and follow the left-hand field boundary. At the end of the hedge, cross a double planked bridge and bear right towards the right-hand side of a large manor house on the hill. Cross another wooden bridge and go straight ahead to emerge onto the main road through the village of Brent Knoll.

The nine-legged lighthouse on Burnham beach

5. Turn right onto the main road and then left into Church Lane. Head straight up the hill before you. As the road bears left, take the kissing gate on your right onto the path signposted to 'The Knoll'. The path forks just as you arrive at the back of the church. Take the left-hand path. After passing through another kissing gate, ignore the stile to your left and continue uphill.

The 450 ft high knoll was once an Iron Age hill fort and was occupied by both Saxons and Romans. Brent is possibly derived from the Saxon word Brennan – *to burn. In old Somerset dialect this word was often applied to hill tops where beacons were burned. This would fit well with Brent Knoll which commands far-reaching views to the Mendip Hills, the Quantocks, Glastonbury and south Wales. Nowadays, it acts as a prominent landmark for those travelling along the M5.*

6. After the next kissing gate, the path splits. You will need the path to your left later. Continue straight ahead up the hill to reach the crest of the knoll. Once you have taken in the views, retrace your steps and turn right onto the path you saw earlier, now just in front of the kissing gate. Follow the track to pass through a farm onto the metalled road.

7. Go straight across the road. To your left is a road indicated as 'Private road to Windy Ridge'. To the right of this there is a courtesy parking area at the end of which is a gate. Pass through the gate and follow the well-worn path into the field. In about 50 yards, the field opens out. At this point head diagonally off to your right across the field towards the very top corner where you will cross a stile between the field gate and the back of a private garden.

8. After crossing the stile, follow the left-hand field boundary to another stile. Cross this and descend steeply down to the village, ignoring a stile halfway down on your left.

9. At the road, go straight across into Station Road and then left into Crooked Lane. Follow this until, after crossing the railway line, you arrive at a T-junction.

10. Turn left. At the next T-junction, turn right to head towards the lighthouse. In about ½ mile, the track bears left where a footpath sign points back the way you came. Turn right here off the main track and continue heading towards the lighthouse. This track eventually leads into Brent Broad.

11. At the end of Brent Broad, turn right and immediately left into Shelley Drive.

12. Turn right at the main road and almost immediately left into St Christopher's Way, following the signposted directions to the golf club. At the entrance to the golf club, turn left onto a signposted bridleway and follow this to reach the beach.

13. Turn left at the coast and follow the beach past the nine-legged lighthouse all the way to the Esplanade. This can be recognised by the distinctive concave sea wall along it to protect the town from heavy seas. Take the first flight of steps up through the sea wall and onto the esplanade and turn right to walk towards the pier.

14. Turn left at the pier into College Street. After crossing the High Street, French's Café Bar will be found on your left.

Walk 11
BREAN DOWN

*B*rean *Down is an outcrop of the Mendip Hills projecting like a finger pointing from the Somerset coastline into the Bristol Channel. This mile-long turf-covered promontory was once an island and occupied by the Romans who had a quayside here. Apart from the initial short uphill stretch, this circuit offers easy walking with far-reaching views along the Somerset coast and across the channel to south Wales. At the far end of the headland there are the remains of a fort dating back to Napoleonic times. On the cliff sides can be found a herd of wild mountain goats. The walk starts and finishes alongside the Brean Down Tropical Bird Garden.*

 Brean Down Tropical Bird Garden was established in 1972 and a visit can conveniently be combined with your walk. The teashop here, which is open to the public, offers a large seated area both inside and out. The menu reflects the seaside nature of this café with a variety of hot and cold food available every day from Easter to October and at weekends during the rest of the year (closed on Christmas Day). Cream teas are also served. Open from 10 am to 4 pm. Telephone: 01278 751209.

Cream teas are also available at the Brean Down Cove Café on the nearby beach. They are open from 9 am to 6 pm every weekend all year round, weather permitting. In the summer season, they are open seven days a week. Telephone: 01278 751088.

If both tea rooms are closed, then refreshments can be found in the centre of Brean, mainly around the Pontin's complex about a mile south of the Down.

DISTANCE: 2¾ miles.
MAP: OS Explorer 153 Weston-Super-Mare and Bleadon Hill.
STARTING POINT: The car park at the Brean Down Tropical Bird Garden (GR 297585).
HOW TO GET THERE: From Burnham-on-Sea, take the B3140 through Berrow and continue northwards to Brean. Go to the very end of this road, past the caravan parks, to the Brean Down Tropical Bird Garden. The car park here is intended for the use of patrons of the garden or teashop. Should the car park be full, there is alternative parking at the beach by the Brean Down Cove Café (there is a charge).

THE WALK
NB: The route is simple but walkers are advised to keep well away from the steep cliff faces. This is quite easy as there are wide, flat and open grass areas throughout the walk. Dogs should be kept on a lead or under close control in the cliff areas.

1. From the car park, walk past the Bird Garden, keeping it on your right. Before you, you will see a concrete stepped path, complete with handrail, leading up onto the Down. Take this path to the very top.

As you reach the top of the path, the view north along the Somerset coastline opens up before you with Weston-Super-Mare staking its claim to the shoreline. When Victoria came to the throne, this was a small and simple fishing village with a handful of families. It is now one of Somerset's largest towns. Projecting into the sea from the Weston sea front are the pier and beyond that Birnbeck Island.

2. Turn left at the top of the path and simply follow the trackway that runs along the ridge of the Down.

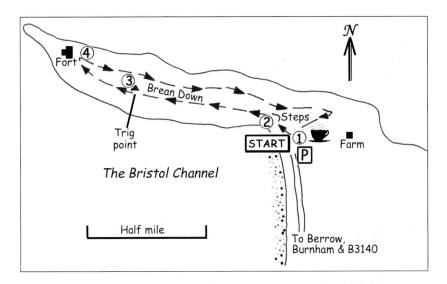

There is plenty of scope along here for observing a variety of sea birds. Peregrine falcons can often be seen and, projecting into the channel as it does, the Down is a popular location for summer migrants at either end of the summer season.

3. In about ¾ mile you will reach a stone triangulation point at the crest of a hill.

Before you, and to the left, is the island of Steep Holm beyond which can be seen the industrial landscape of Barry in South Wales. The island to the right of Steep Holm is Flat Holm with its lighthouse. Slightly to the right of Flat Holm can be seen the white-fronted buildings of Penarth and Cardiff with the Black Mountains beyond.

Continue in the same direction past the triangulation point and before long the old military fort will come into view. The path splits and the choice is yours. Both routes lead down to the fort.

4. Enter the fort and wander around to explore the various military remains.

The fort dates back to the 1860s and was part of the defences against the expected invasion of Napoleon III. It was one of a number built under the orders of the Prime Minister, Lord Palmerston. Others were built, one across the channel at Lavernock Point and two more on the islands of

53

Wild goats on Brean Down

Steep and Flat Holm. The fort is situated 60 ft above sea level and is accessed over a 12 ft dry moat. As you enter, on the left is the guardroom, quarters for two NCOs and twenty men. To the right is the accommodation for four officers plus the kitchen. Beyond these are further buildings, which surround the parade ground and include the gun positions and magazine. Seven muzzle-loaded 7 inch guns, each weighing 7 tons, once looked out over the channel. Or they did until 1900!

Unfortunately there was a major explosion here in 1900 when a Gunner Haines, who was stationed here, allegedly fired a shot directly into the magazine. It was 5 am when the magazine blew up destroying two gun positions and part of the outer wall. Huge coping stones of a hundredweight each were blown 200 yards from the blast. Just one officer was wounded but poor Gunner Haines was blown to pieces.

After this the fort was converted to a tea room which is how it was used until the Second World War. What a shame it isn't open today. In the year 2000, the National Trust bought the dilapidated remains of the fort at the bargain price of £1 and commenced a restoration programme, the results of which you can see.

Return along the tarmac Military Road, which leads you all the way back to the Bird Garden.

Walk 12
SAND BAY

This is an easy walk along a limestone headland that reaches out into the Bristol Channel to the north of Weston-Super-Mare. The circuit starts and finishes at the National Trust car park at the northern end of Sand Bay. Below the cliffs, down in the bay, large mud flats can be seen, green from the growth of glasswort which thrives on these salt marshes.

 Grandma's Tea Rooms at 81 Beach Road in Sand Bay will be found on the coast road on your way to the National Trust car park. A range of hot and cold drinks is offered, alongside cakes, sandwiches, baguettes, ploughman's, soups and jacket potatoes. Also, of course, cream teas. Tables are positioned outside on the forecourt as well as inside. There is a car parking area just to the south. The tea rooms are open daily from mid March to the end of October, 10 am to 5 pm. Telephone: 01934 415228.

When Grandma's is closed, tea is available at The Cliffs, which can be found on the toll road between Sand Bay and the north end of Weston-Super-Mare. This teashop, which, as the name suggests, is perched on the cliffside overlooking the Bristol Channel, is open every day, all year, even Christmas Day, from 10 am to 5.30 pm. Telephone: 01934 420088.

DISTANCE: 2½ miles.

MAP: OS Explorer 153 Weston-Super-Mare and Bleadon Hill.

STARTING POINT: The National Trust car park at the north end of Sand Bay (GR 330659).

HOW TO GET THERE: From junction 21 of the M5, head for Weston-Super-Mare and then follow signs for Sand Bay, which is well signposted all the way. On reaching the coast, turn right and proceed north to the end of the road where the National Trust car park will be found. On your way you will pass Grandma's Tea Rooms on your right-hand side as you travel along this stretch of the coast road.

THE WALK

1. Leave the car park and cross the road to ascend the steps to the right of the public toilets. When the path splits to pass either side of a low overgrown wall, take the path to the left and continue uphill. After passing through a sprung gate, you emerge onto a grass-covered down. Continue in the same direction towards and beyond the triangulation point.

Just before the triangulation point is an interpretation panel which shows your route plus some alternatives you may wish to try.

2. Continue along the path until reaching the rocky headland at Sand Point.

There are fine views to your left across Sand Bay. Birnbeck Island stands just off the coast marking the point where Weston-Super-Mare lies just around the corner. Between you and the distant headland lie large mudflats where wildfowl and waders can frequently been seen. Note the two islands before you, Flat Holm to the right with the lighthouse and Steep Holm to the left.

3. On reaching the rocky headland, retrace your steps and look for the path that runs along the left-hand side of the down between the shore and the ridge of the down. Take this path and follow it to a gate in a stone wall.

Fishermen can often be seen fishing off the rocks here. Mostly it's whiting and codling that make up their catches. Caution needs to be exercised along this stretch of path since there is a long drop down the cliff. It is advisable to keep dogs on a lead along here. For those who prefer not to

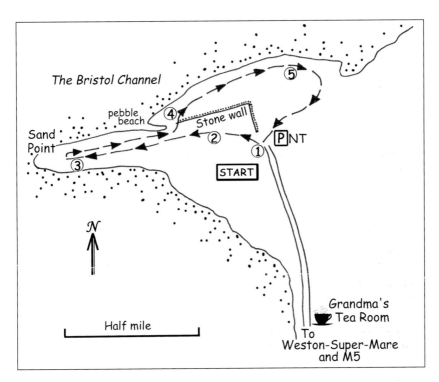

follow a cliffside path, simply retrace your steps back to the triangulation point and continue back to the car park.

4. Pass through the gate into a field with the coast on one side and a long stone wall on the other.

It is possible at this point to climb down over the rocks and explore the pebbled beach. From beach level, the layers of different rock can be seen in the side of the cliff.

Continue along across the field. You can now walk with a more comforting distance between you and the cliff edge.

The very flat stretch you are now crossing, which is so different from the rest of the down area, was once at beach level when the sea was some 15 ft higher than at present.
An alternative and shorter way back is to follow the stone wall to its end where it turns right by a cattle trough. Just around the corner is a gateway,

The rocky headland of Sand Point affords far-reaching views

which takes you back onto the common where the triangulation point can be found. Turning left here will take you back down to the car park.

5. Continue on, keeping the coastline to your left. Pass to the left of the large hillocks to reach and cross a ruined wall, and then bear right to climb a green track.

Looking northwards from here, the views take in Clevedon Pier and, weather permitting, the Severn Bridge.

Approaching the fence line, turn right to re-cross the wall.

The ruins of Woodspring Priory can be seen to the left. Dating from the 1220s, it was dedicated to St Thomas à Becket and is thought to have been built as an act of penance by one of those involved in his death. The property is now in the hands of the National Trust.

Follow the path in the general direction of Birnbeck Island to cross a stile and descend the steps, at the bottom of which is the car park.

Walk 13
CHEW MAGNA AND STANTON DREW

This interesting circuit, which offers easy walking, takes us from the village of Chew Magna, a former cloth town with some wonderful 15th to 17th century buildings, to the neighbouring village of Stanton Drew, famous for its standing stones. The route crosses a medieval bridge with three pointed arches over the River Chew, and takes in two sets of standing stones. Two inns are passed on the way, the Druid's Arms at Stanton Drew, and the Pony and Trap at New Town, both offering alternative starting points for the walk.

The Moondance Tea Rooms can be found right opposite the car park behind the Pelican Inn in Chew Magna. There are pavement tables to the front, as well as a tea garden to the rear and alternative seating within. Cream teas and speciality coffees are served, also a good choice of cold food: quiches and sandwiches and a variety of other light snacks. The tea rooms are open from Monday to Saturday all year round (closed during Christmas week), 10 am to 4.30 pm except on Mondays when they close at 1 pm. Telephone: 01275 331173.

When the Moondance is closed, an alternative (although not on the route of the walk) is the Chew Valley Lake Tea Shop situated on Wallycourt Road in the neighbouring village of Chew Stoke. A wide choice of sandwiches, hot and cold lunches, cakes and cream teas are on offer. Open daily all year round, except Christmas Day and New Year's Day, from 10.30 am to 5.30 pm, 4.30 pm from November to mid-March. Telephone: 01275 333345.

DISTANCE: 5½ miles.
MAP: OS Explorer 155 Bristol & Bath, Keynsham & Marshfield.
STARTING POINT: The free public car park behind the Pelican Inn in Chew Magna (GR 576630).
HOW TO GET THERE: Chew Magna is on the B3130, which runs between the A37 and A38 to the south of Bristol. It is easily spotted on any map, being just to the north of Chew Valley Lake. There is normally reasonable on-street parking available should the public car park be full.
ALTERNATIVE STARTING POINTS: The walk could begin and end at the either of the two inns on the route, the Druid's Arms (point 8) or the Pony and Trap (point 13), both of which have car parks for use of patrons.

THE WALK

1. From the car park, return to the main street and across the road you will see the Moondance Tea Rooms. Just across to the right is the village church. Take the path into the churchyard and bear right, where the path splits, to cross a low stone stile.

2. Continue along the gravelled driveway with Chew Court on your right-hand side and follow the tree-lined path down to the road.

3. Across the road is a field entrance with a stile marked with a footpath sign. Go over the stile into this field, following the sign, and keep to the left-hand field boundary to cross the field. Go over two further stiles, which come close together, and continue in the same direction.

4. When you emerge into a triangular shaped open area, turn left here, keeping the tree-lined River Chew on your left-hand side. As the track approaches a field gate, turn right before the gate, keeping to the left field boundary until reaching a stile on your left, which you cross to enter the field. A waymark sign on this stile points you diagonally across to the right to a wooden stile and stone bridge at the bottom of the field. Cross the stile and bridge and in a few yards turn right onto the farm lane.

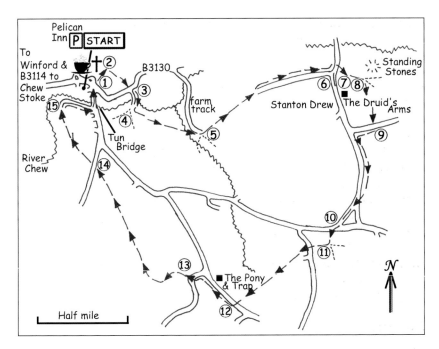

5. The lane bears left and, on the bend, footpath signs tempt you to enter a field. Ignore these and just continue along the lane (Sandy Lane) until reaching the village of Stanton Drew.

6. Turn right at the Lecture Hall where you will see the Druid's Arms just around the corner.

In the gardens of the Druid's Arms you can find the standing stones known as the Cove. These are believed to date back some four to five thousand years, and were probably a Bronze Age ritualistic site.

7. After retracing your steps from the inn, pass the Lecture Hall and keep straight on, turning right at The Cottage just after Sandy Lane. Keep to the right as you go around the corner. You will see a farm gate to your left, next to which a signpost points to the Stone Circles. Pass through the stile by the farm gate to proceed along the tarmac farm road towards the barns.

From here you can see the three stone circles creating a smaller version of Stonehenge. The Great Circle is by the River Chew and originally consisted of 30 stones.

These standing stones can be found in the gardens of the Druid's Arms

8. On reaching the second field gate, the road continues down towards the village sewage plant. Turn right here just before the gate, keeping the field boundary on your left. In a short distance cross a stile marked with a footpath sign, with a line of houses uphill before you. Continue towards the houses, keeping to the right of the field boundary until you emerge onto the road alongside the junior school.

9. Turn right onto the road and then turn left at the T-junction, signposted to Chelwood and Bath. Follow this road, taking the right fork just after a telephone box.

10. On reaching the next road junction, head for the stile opposite, crossing this and veering to the right to cross to the next stile. Follow the path from here up into the wood.

11. Enter the wood over the stile and follow the path through to reach a road. Go straight across at the road, following the footpath signs. Keep heading in the same direction across two fields, keeping the farm and the field boundary to your left, to reach a metalled road.

12. Turn right onto the road and then left shortly after the Pony and Trap pub, signposted to Knowle Hill.

13. After a left-handed bend, turn right (ignoring the road into Tump Cottage) onto a footpath, signposted with '3 Peaks' logos, onto a bracken-covered hill. Follow the metalled road until shortly after Fern Cottage, where it forks. The left-hand path leads down to a house. Do not go down to the house but find the path leading to the left around the back of the house. To do this, at the fork, turn to the left to follow a grass path up through the bracken towards the crest of the hill.

In a short distance, a grass path crosses yours and here you turn right and head along the path through the bracken towards a high hedge. Approaching the hedge, bear right and downhill to find a gate leading onto a path which runs tightly along the 6 ft wooden fence of the private house. In a short distance, pass through a kissing gate and continue straight ahead with the field boundary to your right. Cross a stile into the next field and continue in the same direction, ignoring a farm track that crosses your path, until reaching a metalled road.

14. Your footpath now continues in the same direction straight across the road before you. However, to reach it you must turn left and go 30 yards up the road to where a narrow path leads you back on yourself up the opposite bank. Once you have retraced the 30 yards, but along the top of the bank, you reach two stiles. Take the left one of these. Head downhill, keeping the field boundary to your right. Go over the next stile and then go diagonally down across the field to your left to pick up a stile and a bridge in the bottom corner of the field.

15. Cross the stile and bridge to emerge into a short lane. At the end of this, turn right again and follow this road to a fork where 'Dragons Lane' is shown on a street nameplate. Turn left at this fork and, in a short distance, turn left again at the T-junction with the main road. This leads you over the medieval Tun Bridge with its three pointed arches. You are now heading back up towards the church where your walk started. At the next junction, turn left to find your car park on your left and the Moondance Tea Rooms on your right.

Walk 14
CHEDDAR

Cheddar Gorge is justifiably famous for its towering cliffs and spectacular rock formations. The best way to explore is on foot, avoiding the bustling crowds of Cheddar itself. Millennia ago the effects of running water carved out this awesome landscape from the limestone rocks, forming shapes that allow one's imagination to conjure up countless images. On these rock faces live mountain goats and rare plants such as Alpine pennygrass and the Cheddar pink. Similar actions of the watercourses underground have carved huge caverns, some of which are open to the public and well worth a visit. The initial climb from Cheddar up onto the Mendips is a bit strenuous, gaining almost 700 ft in height, but the effort is rewarded with a wonderful walk and spectacular views.

Set alongside the river, the Edelweiss restaurant is passed as you set out on the walk, and again at the end. The home-made faggots and sausages are a speciality here, also the range of home-baked cakes. Both hot and cold meals are served and the Edelweiss has a reputation for its roast meals, which makes this a particularly popular venue. Cream teas are available too. One can sit either inside or out. From Easter to September the opening hours are 10 am to 5 pm daily, except Mondays and Thursdays when they close at 2 pm. In February, March, October and November the restaurant is open at lunchtimes every day until about 3.30 pm (again 2 pm on Mondays and Thursdays). Telephone: 01934 742347.

Alternatively, the Wishing Well Tea Rooms are passed just a little further along your route and are open daily, 10 am to 5 pm, from March to October, and on Sundays in February and November.

DISTANCE: 5 miles.
MAP: OS Explorer 141 Cheddar Gorge and the Mendip Hills West.
STARTING POINT: The car park next to the Riverside Inn (GR 461535).
HOW TO GET THERE: Cheddar is easily found on the A371 between Axbridge and Wells. From the main road, follow the signs for the gorge and the B3135. This will lead to the pay and display car park next to the Riverside Inn. There are other car parks too; all are well signposted. Some roadside parking can be found in the gorge but be aware of potential rock falls.

THE WALK

☕ **1.** From the car park, turn right and follow the road up through the lower part of the Cheddar Gorge, through the tourist shops and passing the Edelweiss and the Wishing Well Tea Rooms, until reaching a small reservoir on the left-hand side immediately after the Cox's Mill Hotel.

2. A little further along on the left, almost opposite the tourist information office (GR 466539), turn left immediately in front of Rose Cottage and follow the track ahead, passing two more cottages on your left. In a short distance there will be a driveway in front of you leading to a cottage. The path bears right, just before the driveway, taking you behind the cottages. Your route slopes back up the hill to the right.

3. Follow the path steeply uphill as it takes you through a wooded area. The path is obvious and takes you over a stile after which you bear left, continuing your journey uphill to where the woodland starts to thin out. You will see a stile on your left-hand side. Cross this and, before you, you will see a stile on the left. Ignore this and instead turn right to continue up the hill. Hidden in the undergrowth on your right is a tumbledown stone wall. Keep to a straight track up this hill, ignoring all turns to the left and right (even if they are signposted 'Gorge Walk'), until you reach a flagstone stile in a stone wall.

4. Crossing this stile, continue along the same line of direction, keeping

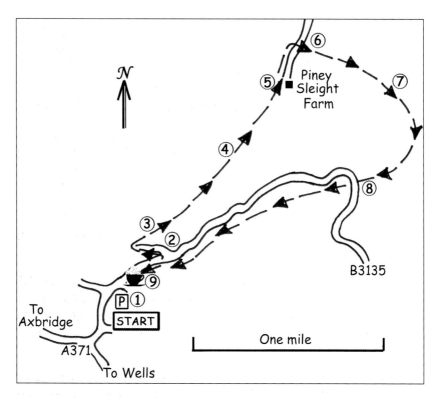

N
Piney Sleight Farm
To Axbridge
A371
To Wells
START
P
One mile
B3135

the field boundary to your left for the next three fields until Piney Sleight Farm comes into view.

5. Keep to the left of the buildings, crossing over two stone stiles at either side of a field adjacent to one of the houses. After the second stile, look to your right for the field gate, beyond which is a metalled farm drive. Take this road, keeping the same line of direction as before for about 300 yards to where a signpost marks the West Mendip Way.

6. Turn right at the signpost to follow the West Mendip Way in the direction of Cheddar. Keeping the field boundary on your right hand side, follow the path until it enters Long Wood.

7. Stay with the downhill path until it merges with another path, which continues down through Black Rock Gorge. Keep to the main track for about ½ mile until you come out onto the B3135 Cheddar road (GR 482544).

Climbers in Cheddar Gorge

Black Rock Nature Reserve is in the ownership of the Somerset Wildlife Trust and consists of 183 acres of mixed habitat in a limestone valley. Watch out for the remains of the old limekiln at Black Rock quarry. The limestone was used to produce lime for spreading on the fields across the Mendips.

8. Cross the road and ascend the signposted track up the opposite side of the gorge in the direction of Cheddar. As you approach the end of the uphill climb, cross over a stile and immediately after the path splits, take the more prominent path to the left, following the line of the fence.

This path takes you all the way along the top of the gorge, with spectacular views. It is a good idea to keep dogs on a lead along this part of the route. For those who suffer from vertigo, just keep to the left, well away from the edge. For those of a more confident disposition – please be aware that the cliff edges are unfenced and there are sheer drops of several hundred feet!

Caution: ignore the distinct left turn to Draycott. Continue along this path until you reach a high metal-framed observation tower at the top of a flight of 300 steps (Jacob's Ladder), which leads down into Cheddar.

9. At the bottom of these steps, pass through the turnstile, turn left and retrace your steps back towards the car park. The Edelweiss and the Wishing Well Tea Rooms will both be found on your left.

Walk 15
WESTHAY

This is a 'lazy day' route, being just 3 miles of flat and easy trails across the Somerset peat moors, which teem with wildlife. Roe deer, herons and wildfowl are all likely to be seen. The walk can easily be combined with a visit to the Peat Moors Visitor Centre – and tea in the adjacent garden centre – a short drive south of Westhay in Shapwick Heath.

Alongside the Peat Moors Visitor Centre in Shapwick Road, and sharing the same parking area, you will find the Willows Tea Rooms at the Willows Garden Centre. Open throughout the year (except for 3 weeks at Christmas) the tea rooms serve a range of hot and cold home-cooked food, including roast dinners and daily specials. Home-made cakes and cream teas are also on offer. The opening times are 9 am to 4.45 pm every day except Sunday when they open at 10 am. Telephone: 01458 860060. And for a new experience, try the 'organic toilets' here. It's not as bad as it sounds but shows how recycling is a serious concern in remote areas.

DISTANCE: 3 miles.

MAP: OS Explorer 141 Cheddar Gorge and Mendip Hills West.

STARTING POINT: The Somerset Wildlife Trust car park between Westhay and Godney (GR 456437).

HOW TO GET THERE: Westhay is a village to the west of Glastonbury on the B3151. From the centre of Westhay, take the B3151 towards Wedmore. In ⅓ mile, turn right at Turnpike House, signposted 'Godney 2¾'. In 1¼ miles, the road bears sharp left and then right. Where it bends right, go straight ahead onto a stoned track (Dagg's Lane Drove) to the parking area just on the right hand side. If necessary, parking along the drove adjacent to the car park is possible, but please ensure that you leave room for agricultural vehicles.

THE WALK

1. Leaving the parking area, turn right onto Dagg's Lane Drove to head towards the Mendip Hills, keeping the high pylons behind you.

To your left is the Decoy Pool, which is just one of the many large expanses of water along this walk. The whole area consists of peat moors and shows signs of the effects of the commercial extraction of peat. Over recent decades, the importance of this region as a nationally significant reserve for wildlife has been recognised. You can expect to see herons and mallards at least and hear the occasional burst of song from Cetti's warblers. If you are extremely lucky, you may glimpse a rare and shy otter, a species that appears to be making a comeback. Beautifully marked jays can often be spotted along the edge of the woodland area.

2. In 400 yards, turn left through a Somerset Wildlife Trust gate signed as 'Foot access to London Drove and Hides'.

The hide before you is generally open to the public and offers the visitor views across the reed beds. Please enter quietly as others may already be inside observing the wildlife through the narrow observation windows. Also inside, and worth a visit in their own right, are a number of interpretation panels that explain the way the peat moors have been excavated and now serve as a wildlife haven.

Continue past the hide and follow the trail to its end, ignoring all side tracks along the way.

To your right are large areas of water and reed beds. To the left you can see alders and willows, which thrive in this wet habitat and support a

69

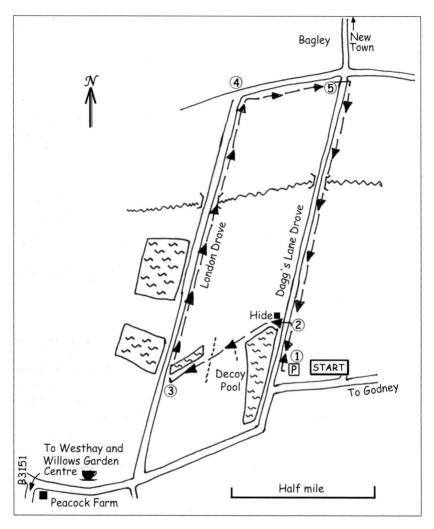

great deal of wildlife. Badgers and foxes abound, and in the summer months magnificent dragonflies hover over the water and occasionally fall prey to the hobby, a summer-visiting small bird of prey, which flies low over the moors taking small creatures on the wing.

3. Arriving at the end of the track, pass through the kissing gate and turn right onto the stone-covered London Drove.

Extensive peat workings can be seen along this drove. The peat has been

70

A reconstruction of a circular Iron Age dwelling

formed over several thousands of years by the slow decay of vegetable matter in the acid waters. Traditionally peat was dug by hand into chunks, between the size of a brick and a breezeblock. These pieces of peat were stacked into beehive shaped stands called ruckles, and there left to dry. They provided a reasonable source of fuel and were a significant form of heating in my family's home in the days of my childhood.

In recent years, the fashion for gardening has led to the extensive removal of peat for sale in garden centres and the extraction has outstripped all previous expectations. Peat digging machines carve out trenches about 3 ft across and 2 ft deep in contrast to the days when it was hand dug. To make extraction easier, the levels are also drained of water and this causes conflict for the conservationists who require a high water table.

4. On reaching the metalled road at the end of this drove, turn right and follow the road for about 600 yards until you pick up the far end of Dagg's Lane Drove.

5. Turn right into Dagg's Lane Drove, which leads in a straight line back to your car park.

Walk 16
WOOKEY HOLE

Wookey Hole is, of course, famous for its caves, which have yielded remains of rhinoceros, wolf and early man. This walk – best saved for a dry spell – combines a hilltop path across the Mendip ridge with the small (by Cheddar Gorge standards) but impressive Ebbor Gorge and tea in the village of Wookey Hole. It is a lovely route and well worth the effort of the climb through the gorge.

 The Old Bakery Tea Rooms can be found tucked away behind the Homestead Stores in the village of Wookey Hole. An interesting range of hot and cold food is on offer, most of it home-cooked. Both indoor and outdoor seating is available, looking down across a well-kept garden. The tea rooms are open on Saturday to Wednesday from Easter to the end of September, 10.30 am to 5.30 pm. Telephone: 01749 673169.

Alternatively, the Galloper Family Restaurant, which is part of the Wookey Hole Visitor Centre and is situated on the edge of the car park, is open all year. It is a large and airy indoor facility seating over 100. There is a wide range of self-service food available including cream teas, hot and cold meals and drinks. Open seven days a week from 10.30 am to 5.30 pm in the winter and 6.30 pm in the summer. In the winter months, the large restaurant closes and a smaller coffee shop area opens up in the nearby gift shop. Closing times in the winter may depend on the time of the last visitor entry into the caves. Telephone: 01749 672243.

DISTANCE: 3 miles.
MAP: OS Explorer 141 Cheddar Gorge and Mendip Hills West.
STARTING POINT: The free car park at the Wookey Hole Visitor Centre (GR 532475). This car park is only for the use of visitors to the caves. Walkers can justify its use by combining this walk with a trip underground. For those who have not been here before, it is well worth the experience.
HOW TO GET THERE: Wookey Hole can be reached from the A371. As a tourist attraction, it is well signposted from the city of Wells. The car park is a large one and easily found. If you are not also visiting the caves, there is a limited amount of roadside parking available.

THE WALK
NB: The main route through Ebbor Gorge includes a steep climb where in places you may well find yourself using your hands as well as feet. It is a well trodden route and hence the rocks can be slippery in wet weather as a result of centuries of feet grinding them down to a smooth surface. An alternative path is also described below, but this will miss the spectacle of the gorge!

1. On leaving the car park, turn left along the road, past Ebbor House, until reaching on the right-hand side an unnamed bungalow where a signed gatepost indicates the bridleway to Priddy (3 miles). Turn right here through the gateway onto an obvious stony track.

2. Shortly after, bear left where the path splits to go through a wooded valley.

3. In about 400 yards, cross a stile to enter the English Nature Reserve of Ebbor Gorge.

Just inside the gate, an interpretation panel gives the layout of the reserve area.

Continue along the distinct path, ignoring the first path off to the right signposted to Priddy (although this could provide an easier alternative route as described below).

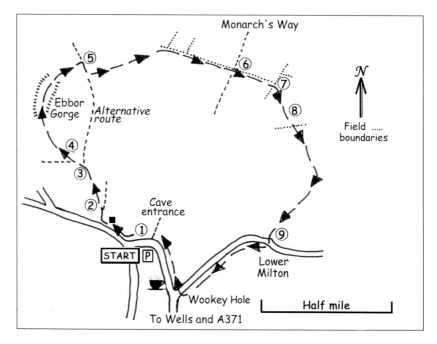

The alternative path provides easier walking but you will miss the gorge itself. On this route, follow the path to a T-junction where you will eventually go right but first take a detour to the left for 50 yards to a spectacular clifftop viewpoint. Caution – there is a sheer drop at the edge!

Retracing your steps, continue straight ahead at the point where you previously turned left, and continue to a point where a path joins from your left. Continue straight ahead. The path from your left is the main route rejoining (see * in point 5 below).

4. For the main route, take the next right, just a few yards further along, signposted to the gorge. The next stage involves a steep climb, in places 45°. However, it is not precipitous, just steep.

5. At the end of the gorge path, you will reach a T-junction of paths where a fallen tree provides a convenient resting place. Turn right here in the direction marked 'Car Park'. Shortly after, at the next T-junction, turn left* and continue the uphill climb out of the Ebbor Gorge Nature Reserve by crossing a stile.

* You may prefer to turn right here and cover the short distance to a viewpoint before retracing your steps and picking up the route once again.

Continue straight on, keeping the field boundary on your left, across three hilltop fields.

6. Immediately after crossing a field boundary, you will see a stile made of rocks and round metal horizontal bars in the field boundary wall on your left. This indicates where the Monarch's Way crosses your path at right angles.

You could, if you wish to cut short your trip, turn right here and follow this footpath all the way down into Wookey Hole. Keeping the field boundaries on your right, as you cross each field along this waymarked route, you should be able to see the next stile before you. Cross three fields in this fashion until in the fourth and final field, you will bear right towards a stand of fir trees where the path comes out onto a metalled road by a nursing home. Turn right here and in a short distance, you reach the Wookey Hole Visitor Centre. By turning left here, you will pass the car park on your right and in a short distance the Old Bakery Tea Rooms.

Continue across one more field until you reach a six-bar gate with a wooden stile on its right-hand side.

7. Here you need to head diagonally off to the right across this field. This takes you downhill towards the hedge line on the lower edge of the field. This path is often indistinct but it is there as a right of way. If in doubt, your compass bearing is 160°.

8. This leads you down to another six-bar gate with a wooden stile to its left. Cross this into a well-defined lane, which passes through woodland and fields down to the metalled road.

9. Turn right at the road and then right at the T-junction and before long you will reach Wookey Hole and the Old Bakery Tea Rooms. Just a short distance further brings you back to the car park.

Wookey Hole caves receive a third of a million visitors per year. In addition to the caves, the attraction includes part of the Madame Tussaud's waxwork collection and a paper mill where you can make your own paper.

Walk 17
GLASTONBURY

*T*his route, which offers easy walking and has no major ascents, takes in
some fine views across the Somerset peat moors to Wells and the southern
face of the Mendip Hills. The path you tread has been crossed by pilgrims
for at least 2,000 years. For much of the way round, the notable landmark
of Glastonbury Tor, famous through Arthurian legend, is in view. It is
worth considering how the high ground on which you walk was once an
island when the sea reached well inland from its present position.

The popular and much-loved Abbey Tea Rooms will be found at 16 Magdalene Street, opposite the abbey ruins car park. There is a wonderfully traditional atmosphere here with waitress service, linen tablecloths and fresh flowers on the tables, all providing a real 'Miss Marples' image of the old-world English teashop. They are open every day (except Christmas Day) from 10 am to 5 pm, offering morning coffees followed by home-cooked lunches with a wide choice of daily specials, including a roast on Sunday. Traditional afternoon teas are served and there is a large selection of memorable home-made cakes. Telephone: 01458 832852.

DISTANCE: 4 miles.
MAP: OS Explorer 141 Cheddar Gorge and Mendip Hills West.
STARTING POINT: The pay and display car park in Silver Street, Glastonbury (GR 500389).
HOW TO GET THERE: Glastonbury is easily found on the A39 between Bridgwater and Wells. Should the Silver Street car park be full, other pay and display parking is well signposted from the High Street.

THE WALK
1. From the car park, turn right and then almost immediately left into the short side street that leads out into the High Street. Remember this little lane for your return route back to the car park.

There is a mystical and magical feel to Glastonbury. Many religions can be found being practised here and the shops reflect the variety of persuasions present in the town with herbal remedies, alternative medicines and books on the occult. House windows passed on your route will give clues to the pacifist and green nature of many of the members of the Glastonbury community.

2. Turn right onto the High Street, going uphill to the top of the road. Continue in the same uphill direction into Bove Town along which will be found many homes of members of the peace community.

3. Bear right into Wick Hollow and continue uphill, past Bulwark Lane.

Walking up this lane, deeply cut into the hillside, notice the magnificent tree roots which have been exposed by erosion over the centuries and provide a strong feeling of the underworld.

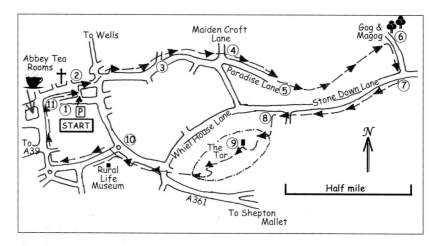

4. You come to a T-junction with Maiden Croft Lane on the left. From here you can view Glastonbury Tor to your right. Go straight on from here onto the dirt track path by crossing the stile. This is locally known as Paradise Lane and is indicated by a footpath sign (GR 512392). Pass over another stile and keep the hedge boundary on your right-hand side, then another stile and continue to keep the hedge on your right.

Along here there are magnificent views to your left across to the Mendips and the city of Wells.

5. Where the path splits, take the right-hand path through a kissing gate and continue straight ahead, keeping the hedge boundary on your left. In a short distance, you will pass through another kissing gate, still keeping the hedge boundary on your left, and descend down the hill, veering slightly to your right to pass through a hedgerow by crossing a stile. Follow the path downhill in the next field until you emerge onto a green lane.

As you descend, notice ahead of you the two ancient oak trees, now quite dead, known as Gog and Magog. These are probably around a 1,000 years old.

6. Turn right onto the green lane and continue until reaching the metalled road.

7. Turn right here to travel uphill to a T-junction where you will turn

Glastonbury Tor

right and then almost immediately after turn left through a gate onto the very obvious path to the top of Glastonbury Tor.

8. Follow the path all the way to the top of the Tor.

Allow yourself plenty of time on top of the Tor to take in the views. An engraved compass indicates all the local landmarks that can be viewed on a clear day. It was here that the 80-year-old Richard Whiting, the last Abbot of Glastonbury, was hanged in 1539 on the orders of Thomas Cromwell, having refused to give up the abbey to Henry VIII. The trial took place in nearby Wells where the Abbot sat in the Glastonbury Chair, now to be seen in the Bishop's Palace in Wells. After the execution, the Abbot's body was quartered and the pieces sent to four Somerset towns.

9. Continue your journey down the concrete path on the other side of the Tor. On emerging onto a side road (with a Chalice Well notice before you), turn left and then immediately right onto the main road and head back into Glastonbury town.

The Chalice Well at the base of the Tor produces 25,000 gallons a day. It is in the grounds of a tea garden, which offers an alternative stopping point along your route.

10. At the mini-roundabout turn left, passing the Rural Life Museum, the former abbey barn, on your left-hand side.

The museum, which appeals to all ages, is full of agricultural and rural artefacts and is well worth a visit .

At the next mini-roundabout, turn right, heading downhill and passing the ruins of Glastonbury Abbey on your right-hand side. The Abbey Tea Rooms will be found on your left.

The abbey was once one of the most powerful in the country. Built in AD 688, it was founded on the site of a Saxon wattle church and was eventually dissolved in 1539. The West Saxon King Ine built a stone church here in the late 8th century and this was rebuilt by St Dunstan in the 10th century. King Arthur and Queen Guinevere are said to be buried in the grounds but this appears to have been a medieval public relations exercise to boost the influence of Glastonbury as a centre for pilgrimage. In the grounds can be seen the 14th-century Abbot's Kitchen, a barn for grain storage and a fish store.

11. Continuing down into the town centre, turn right to go up the High Street and about two thirds of the way up you will see the short lane through which you passed earlier and which leads back to your car park.

Walk 18
LANGPORT AND MUCHELNEY

This is a flat 6 mile walk following the meandering banks of the River Parrett. It begins at the Saxon settlement of Langport and passes through dairy meadowland with herds of Friesian cattle to skirt Muchelney, which is famous for its medieval Benedictine abbey and the John Leach pottery. Although slightly off the route, the village is well worth a visit and a splendid tea can be had here. Alternatively the walk could start at Muchelney, reaching Langport about two-thirds of the way round.

The Almory Café and Stable Tea Rooms, which are part of the same premises, in the village of Muchelney, offer a warm and friendly welcome. Cream teas, light snacks, home-made cakes, hot meals, soups, quiches, baguettes and speciality teas can all be enjoyed whilst viewing the church on one side or the Somerset Levels on the other. Indoor and outdoor seating are both available. The surroundings are very pleasant, the high-ceilinged café area having a galleried landing from which hang various decorative carpets. Large windows provide a light and airy feeling. The opening times are 11 am to 3 pm on Wednesday to Friday and 11 am to 4.30 pm on Saturday and Sunday. Closed from Christmas to the end of January. Telephone: 01458 252560.

In Langport the Parrett Coffee House and Gallery in Bow Street, which is just a matter of yards from the start of the walk, serves home-made cakes, hot croissants and various snacks. This is open from 9.30 am to 4 pm on Monday to Saturday all year (closed for Christmas). Telephone: 01458 251717. When both teashops are closed, the Drayton Arms pub in Drayton would be a source of refreshment.

DISTANCE: 6 miles.
MAP: OS Explorer 129 Yeovil and Sherborne.
STARTING POINT: The free car park at Stacey's Court (GR 416265)
HOW TO GET THERE: Langport can be found on the A378 between Taunton and
    Somerton, or on the A372 between Bridgwater and Yeovil. Travelling from
    Bridgwater or Yeovil, on entering Langport, follow signs for Taunton. This will
    take you onto the A378, Bow Street, along which will be found the car park,
    well signposted on the left-hand side, about 100 yards after the large landmark
    clock. Approaching from Taunton, you enter Bow Street with the car park on
    your right. An alternative car park, through which the route passes (point 2),
    can be found opposite the clock. Limited street parking is also available in side
    streets but the official car parks offer plenty of choice.
ALTERNATIVE STARTING POINT: You could start the walk at Muchelney,
    joining the route at Westover Bridge (see point 5). To reach the village by car,
    just follow the brown tourist signs to Muchelney Abbey. You will find that the
    church, the abbey ruins and the tea rooms, plus a car park, all conveniently
    cluster around the same road junction.

The Walk
Langport was once a walled town and the Hanging Chapel, which dates back to 1353, was the old East Gate. It was a thriving port and a major battle was fought here during the English Civil War when the Royalists were routed. Before leaving they burnt down Bow Street, where the walk begins, and then headed to Bridgwater Castle for safety.

1. On leaving the car park, return to Bow Street and turn right. Before you will be a large clock affixed to a building on the left-hand side. You will also pass the Parrett Coffee House on your right.

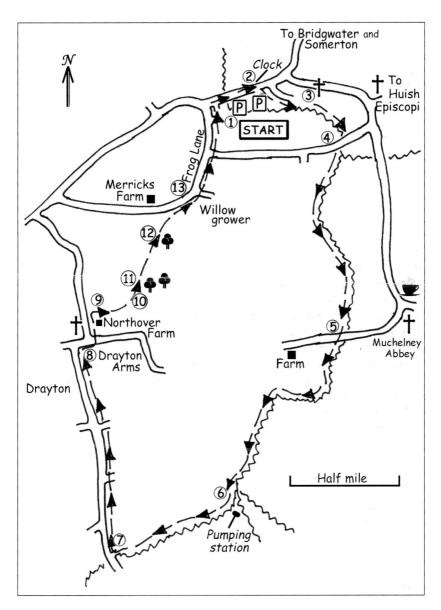

2. At the clock, turn right into the large car park. Walk along the path with the shops on your right. At the end of the path, look left to spot the library and tourist office. Walking past these offices, enter a dead end lane with cottages on the left and bungalows on the right.

The Benedictine Muchelney Abbey

3. At the end of the road, turn right to reach the riverbank where you turn left, following the footpath with the river on your right.

Along here can be seen the fine church towers of Langport, on your left, and Huish Episcopi. A number of towers become visible along this walk and between them represent some of the finest Perpendicular church towers in the county.

4. You will soon reach a small gravel car park where the concrete Huish Bridge crosses the river. Cross over this bridge and turn left to once again follow the riverbank but this time keeping it to your left.

The stretch you now enter is typical of so much of the Somerset landscape, low, flat and almost treeless. Here the fields are divided by large ditches called rhines (pronounced reens) instead of hedgerows. The low-lying fields often flood in winter and offer a suitable habitat for many wading birds and at times large flocks of tumbling lapwings can be seen.

 5. When you reach Westover Bridge, you can divert left for a few hundred yards to the village of Muchelney and the Almory Café and Stable Tea Rooms.

Here you can visit the ancient Muchelney Abbey, adjacent to the tea rooms, and the workshops of John Leach, the famous potter whose work is exhibited and sold worldwide.

To continue the walk, cross the road and stay on the riverbank, with the water still on your left.

You will pass a point where the now disused railway crossed the river. The remains of the old bridge, which once carried the Langport to Yeovil branch of the Somerset and Dorset railway, are still clearly visible.

6. Following the riverside path, and after passing a pumping station on the opposite bank, you eventually reach a metalled road.

7. Turn right on reaching the road and follow this all the way into Drayton village.

8. On reaching a T-junction, turn right. You will find the church on your left and the Drayton Arms on your right. Turn left immediately after the church into North Street.

9. In a short distance, you will come to Northover Farm on your right. Immediately after the farm barn, turn right. A signpost on the barn wall shows this to be the footpath to 'Langport 1 mile'. At the end of the short green track, enter into the field and head for the stile almost straight across in front of you (ignoring the finger sign which points to a footpath to the right).

10. Immediately after crossing the stile, turn left to enter an area of scrub. You will shortly emerge into an open field. Turn right here and follow the footpath, keeping the hedge on your right. On reaching the corner of the field, pass through a small gap in the hedge to reach the next field.

11. Before you, as though in the middle of the field, you will see a small wood. To its right is the church tower of Langport. You will also see three telegraph poles crossing the field in front of you. The middlemost of these will be at the left-hand edge of the woodland. Head for this pole, at the base of which you will find another small gap in the hedge, which takes you into the next field.

12. Follow the footpath, keeping the trees on your right, until reaching the end of the woodland. The next bit can be tricky since the footpath is not always clear thanks to crop planting. It may therefore be necessary to follow the field boundary around to your destination on the far side of the field. Before you and slightly to your left will be seen Merrick's Farm, a cream-coloured building. This is on a track, which leads across in front of it. Further along that track to the right you will see a willow grower's cottage where withy canes can often be seen standing. There are also two poles about 12 ft high with a bar going across the top. This is in the withy grower's yard and it is there that you will find the stile that takes you onto the gravel road. Head diagonally across the field to this stile, or around the field margins if crops dictate.

13. On reaching the road, turn right and continue as it bears left, leading you up into Frog Lane and on to the main road in Langport. Turn right at the main road and in a short distance you will reach your car park on the right-hand side.

Walk 19
MONTACUTE

This lovely ramble, probably best saved for a fine day, takes in a selection of the hills in south Somerset. The route goes through deciduous woodland and finishes in the splendour of the grounds of Montacute House. Montacute village itself can boast a wonderful collection of soft yellow stone buildings, which attract many a maker of period films.

 The Montacute Country Tea Rooms and their garden are set in the very centre of Montacute, in South Street, and are easily seen from the car park. Hot and cold meals are served, along with a range of home-made cakes, which are a speciality, and of course cream teas. In the summer months, Easter to October, the tea rooms are open from 12.30 pm to 5 pm on Wednesday to Saturday and 2 pm to 5 pm on Sunday. Please phone for details of winter opening. Telephone: 01935 823024. The Montacute TV and Radio Memorabilia Museum adjoins the teashop and is well worth a visit in its own right, providing a nostalgic trip down Memory Lane with a range of receivers from across the years and children's books and toys based on TV programmes.

DISTANCE: 5½ miles.
MAP: OS Explorer 129 Yeovil and Sherborne.
STARTING POINT: The free car park at The Borough, Montacute (GR 498168).
HOW TO GET THERE: The village of Montacute can be found just south of the A3088 to the west of Yeovil. It is well signposted thanks to Montacute House, a National Trust property. In addition to the car park, there is normally ample on-street parking available.

The Walk
NB: Some parts of this walk can be muddy after wet weather, so be prepared with suitable shoes or boots.

1. From the car park, turn left and go west along Middle Street towards the Kings Arms Inn. Just before the pub, turn left with the church on your left and the old school on your right.

2. Turn right through the gate labelled 'Abbey Farm Private Road'. Walk across the yard to the gate and cross the stile. Once past the gate, bear left to find a sunken track passing up through the trees. In about 200 yards, the path emerges into an open field.

Abbey Farm was the former gatehouse to Montacute Priory.

3. Bear right here to cross the stile into the woods adjoining the field. Now simply follow the steep path up St Michael's Hill. The path leads to a T-junction onto a gravel path. Turn left here and follow the path to the summit of the hill.

This steep uphill path can be slippery when wet. At the bottom, it is possible to choose a path with a lesser incline, which works its way round the hill to the top.

At the summit of the hill there is a tower, which can be ascended with care. It was built as a folly in 1760 by Sir Edward Phelips, the occupant of Montacute House. The Normans had previously built a castle on the summit though no traces remain today.

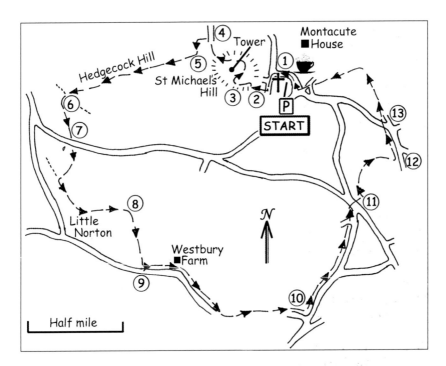

After a visit to the tower, retrace your steps down from the summit. Ignore the path to your right, which is the route you came up earlier, but keep to the path you are on to descend the hill, with the higher ground on your left-hand side. When you come to a field gate with a stile, cross this and bear right to a field gate clearly visible at the bottom end of the field.

4. At the bottom of the field, pass through the gate and turn immediately left onto a vehicle track. At a couple of metal-gated entrances, the path bears left and up into the woods.

5. In about 80 yards, bear right where the path forks.

In the field on your right you may be lucky enough to see an ostrich and a couple of llamas!

You are now walking through shady sycamore woodland, along the right-hand edge of Hedgecock Hill. Just after a derelict pumping house, the path splits into two or three, only to merge again. Ignore a deep gullied

The magnificent Montacute House is well worth visiting

uphill path to your left. Shortly after this, ascend the wooden steps with a handrail and turn right onto the path at the top of the steps. Bear left where the path forks at a sign which points back the way you came from Montacute.

6. Your path emerges at a crossing of paths with standing stones before you. Continue straight on, keeping in the same general direction as before. You will pass a couple of signs on your left warning of steep quarry faces. Shortly after, the path forks and here you bear left and follow the path up to the metalled road.

7. Go straight across the road, following the signpost to Norton sub Hamdon to arrive at a car park. Over to your left you will see a gravelled path, which you follow to exit the car park. A number of paths go off before you but the one you require is to the right of the fenced area and is signposted 'Norton sub Hamdon ½ mile'. In about 40 yards, turn left at the T-junction and continue straight on when two paths merge from your left. Ignore the footpath to Little Norton on your right and continue to a T-junction with a post holding several waymarkers.

8. Turn right here to descend briefly before following the contours and ignoring any paths that drop down to your right.

To your left is a dry valley with evidence of strip lynchets. These are field terraces created by medieval farmers to make ploughing more practical.

After passing through a small clearing, and re-entering the woods, in about 100 yards, go straight on at the crossroads. Your path will now remain in the woods whilst fields are on your left. Follow this gullied path all the way down to the metalled road.

9. Turn left onto the road. Go past Westbury Farm on your left and continue straight on as the road becomes a dirt vehicle track and then only wide enough for walking.

10. In about a mile, turn left at the T-junction and continue along this track, keeping to the left where the path forks. On reaching the metalled road at the entrance to Pitt Plain Farm, bear right to join the next road at a T-junction.

11. Go straight across here onto the grass track towards what appears to be a walled garden but is a burial ground. Turn left over the stile just before the high wall and continue with the wall to your right to cross another stile. Keep to the right-hand field boundary to descend to another stile, which leads you into woodland. Emerging from the trees across another stile, turn left and then bear right to follow the hill contours around in the direction of a tin shed. Your path goes just to the right of the shed, then follows a field boundary with the field on your left.

12. You shortly come to a parallel pair of metalled gates through which you go to emerge onto the road. Turn left here and left again soon after, following the road sign to Montacute.

13. In a short distance, go through the gated drive alongside and to the left of Odcombe Lodge. Follow the drive until you are looking straight ahead at the magnificent Montacute House.

The house is a late 16th-century Elizabethan mansion owned by the National Trust and is well worth a visit. It contains a 44m-long gallery that houses part of the National Portrait Collection. NT members may prefer to walk through the grounds to reach the village centre.

There will be a line of trees to your right and another to your left. Your path now continues through those trees to your left to emerge onto the village road. Turn right at the road towards The Borough, passing the Montacute Country Tea Rooms on your right.

Walk 20
BRUTON

This is an easy circuit from the centre of Bruton. It passes along the back lanes of this small Somerset town affording views of some of Somerset's fine architecture, takes in the Bruton Dovecote, passes through meadowland and finishes with a riverside stroll. The chosen café is just a few yards off the route.

Dovecote Café and Deli is a small teashop at 26 High Street, Bruton. It offers friendly service in cosy, old-style premises. Although conveniently placed, with its entrance in the High Street, the tea room itself is set back away from the main road. Cream teas are available along with a wide range of light lunches and snacks, including teacakes, toasties, sandwiches and home-made cakes, all made from local produce. Open on Monday to Saturday all year except on bank holidays. The hours are 8.30 am to 4.30 pm, with early closing at 1 pm on Thursdays and Saturdays. Telephone: 01749 812782.

When the Dovecote is closed, the nearest alternative tea room I have found is the Old Bakehouse in the High Street at Castle Cary, a few miles south-west of Bruton, next door to the NatWest Bank. This is open all year from 9.30 am on Tuesday to Saturday except at Christmas and for two weeks in February. Last orders are taken at 4 pm. Telephone: 01963 350067.

DISTANCE: 3¾ miles.
MAP: OS Explorer 142 Shepton Mallet and Mendip Hills East.
STARTING POINT: The free car park in Higher Backway (GR 683349).
HOW TO GET THERE: Bruton can be found where the B3081 crosses the A359 between Frome and Yeovil. In the town centre, the Blue Ball Hotel can be found at one end of the High Street at its junction with Coombe Street. Just a few yards up Coombe Street, Higher Backway is a minor road off to the left and the car park is on the right side as you enter this lane. This parking is not signposted from the town centre.

THE WALK
1. On leaving the car park, turn right into Coombe Street and right again into the High Street. In a short distance, turn left into an alleyway named as 'Amos Barton'.

Just before entering the alley, notice Barton's Café and Deli just a few yards along, also on the left-hand side.

Turn right at the end of the alley onto a metalled lane. A small park appears on your left-hand side, which you access through an iron gate and go over the river following the tarmac walkway. On crossing the bridge, notice the steps leading up to the road just at the top of the high ground about 50 yards before you. Follow this tarmac path, up to the steps, to emerge onto the road. Go straight across and bear left, signposted to Godminster. In 50 yards the road bears left but continue straight ahead onto the tarmac footpath. Follow this all the way to the lane's end where you emerge onto the main road. Turn left, pass under the bridge and turn immediately left again into Park Road.

2. Continue uphill along Park Road until the road splits three ways at a junction where a wooden bench seat is placed.

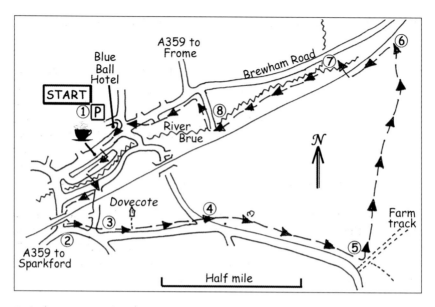

3. Your route is the middle of these three, signposted to Wincanton and Gillingham.

On your left-hand side will be found the almost complete ruins of the Bruton Dovecote. It is now in the ownership of the National Trust.

Continue along this road until reaching the main road with a bungalow at the junction.

4. Go straight across at the main road to cross a stile into the corner of a field. Bear right to go over another stile in just a few yards. Once into the next field, look straight ahead to the woods before you and, with the pond on your right-hand side, walk to the woods ahead, keeping parallel with the main road. This leads you to a stile, which you cross to enter the woods and follow the well-defined track. Where a farm track crosses your path, turn left onto the track, which leads you out of the woods and into a field. Turn right over a stile to return to your previous direction and follow the field boundary, which you will keep on your right. Cross the stile into the next field.

Before proceeding any farther, look to your left to where the hedge through which you have passed runs down to the lower corner of the field. Your exit from the field is down in that corner but that is not the way the official

*footpath runs. Hence you will go straight ahead to a track and then turn
back to head for that corner.*

5. Continue in the same direction walking towards a barn before you.
Part way across the field, a very distinct farm track crosses your path. It is
at this point that you turn left, not to follow the farm track, but to veer off
diagonally left from the farm track to head for the bottom corner of the
field, where you exit the field over a stile. Keeping the small pond on
your left, go straight ahead through the corner of the wood to cross
another stile in about 30 yards. Turn right to go across the field to a stiled
gate at the bottom end. Entering the next field, bear left following the
farm track but bear right off this track when a choice of two gates appears
in the hedge before you. Pass through the right-hand gate of this pair.
Once into the next field, veer slightly right to follow a well-worn track
down to a field gate. This is the first of two gates close together through
which you pass as you cross the narrow river. Continue along this track,
which leads you uphill to the railway embankment.

6. Turn left before the railway lines to follow the footpath with the
railway to your right. The path passes under a railway bridge. Once
through to the other side, turn left into a field, following the obvious path
with the field boundary and river to your left.

7. At the end of the first field, go over the bridge and now follow the
footpath, with the river and field boundary to your right. Cross the next
stile and walk over the wooden bridge. Turn right here to enter the
woods and follow the riverside path all the way to where it emerges onto
a back lane behind a row of houses.

*There are points where it looks as if the path leads away from the river, but
just stick to the riverbank walkway.*

8. Cross the stile into the lane and turn right to follow the lane all
the way up to the main road, where you turn left to walk back into the
town centre, ignoring all turnings to left or right. On reaching the Blue
Ball Hotel, which you passed at the very beginning of your walk, the car
park is just to the right and the teashop to the left.